T0166009

Tremendous Trifles

Tremendous Trifles

G.K. Chesterton

MINT EDITIONS

Tremendous Trifles was first published in 1909.

This edition published by Mint Editions 2021.

ISBN 9781513271521 | E-ISBN 9781513276526

Published by Mint Editions®

 MINT
EDITIONS

minteditionbooks.com

Publishing Director: Jennifer Newens
Design & Production: Rachel Lopez Metzger
Project Manager: Micaela Clark
Typesetting: Westchester Publishing Services

Contents

I

Tremendous Trifles

Once upon a time there were two little boys who lived chiefly in the front garden, because their villa was a model one. The front garden was about the same size as the dinner table; it consisted of four strips of gravel, a square of turf with some mysterious pieces of cork standing up in the middle and one flower bed with a row of red daisies. One morning while they were at play in these romantic grounds, a passing individual, probably the milkman, leaned over the railing and engaged them in philosophical conversation. The boys, whom we will call Paul and Peter, were at least sharply interested in his remarks. For the milkman (who was, I need say, a fairy) did his duty in that state of life by offering them in the regulation manner anything that they chose to ask for. And Paul closed with the offer with a business-like abruptness, explaining that he had long wished to be a giant that he might stride across continents and oceans and visit Niagara or the Himalayas in an afternoon dinner stroll. The milkman producing a wand from his breast pocket, waved it in a hurried and perfunctory manner; and in an instant the model villa with its front garden was like a tiny doll's house at Paul's colossal feet. He went striding away with his head above the clouds to visit Niagara and the Himalayas. But when he came to the Himalayas, he found they were quite small and silly-looking, like the little cork rockery in the garden; and when he found Niagara it was no bigger than the tap turned on in the bathroom. He wandered round the world for several minutes trying to find something really large and finding everything small, till in sheer boredom he lay down on four or five prairies and fell asleep. Unfortunately his head was just outside the hut of an intellectual backwoodsman who came out of it at that moment with an axe in one hand and a book of Neo-Catholic Philosophy in the other. The man looked at the book and then at the giant, and then at the book again. And in the book it said, "It can be maintained that the evil of pride consists in being out of proportion to the universe." So the backwoodsman put down his book, took his axe and, working eight hours a day for about a week, cut the giant's head off; and there was an end of him.

Such is the severe yet salutary history of Paul. But Peter, oddly enough, made exactly the opposite request; he said he had long wished to be a pigmy about half an inch high; and of course he immediately became one. When the transformation was over he found himself in the midst of an immense plain, covered with a tall green jungle and above which, at intervals, rose strange trees each with a head like the sun in symbolic pictures, with gigantic rays of silver and a huge heart of gold. Toward the middle of this prairie stood up a mountain of such romantic and impossible shape, yet of such stony height and dominance, that it looked like some incident of the end of the world. And far away on the faint horizon he could see the line of another forest, taller and yet more mystical, of a terrible crimson colour, like a forest on fire for ever. He set out on his adventures across that coloured plain; and he has not come to the end of it yet.

Such is the story of Peter and Paul, which contains all the highest qualities of a modern fairy tale, including that of being wholly unfit for children; and indeed the motive with which I have introduced it is not childish, but rather full of subtlety and reaction. It is in fact the almost desperate motive of excusing or palliating the pages that follow. Peter and Paul are the two primary influences upon European literature to-day; and I may be permitted to put my own preference in its most favourable shape, even if I can only do it by what little girls call telling a story.

I need scarcely say that I am the pigmy. The only excuse for the scraps that follow is that they show what can be achieved with a commonplace existence and the sacred spectacles of exaggeration. The other great literary theory, that which is roughly represented in England by Mr. Rudyard Kipling, is that we moderns are to regain the primal zest by sprawling all over the world growing used to travel and geographical variety, being at home everywhere, that is being at home nowhere. Let it be granted that a man in a frock coat is a heartrending sight; and the two alternative methods still remain. Mr. Kipling's school advises us to go to Central Africa in order to find a man without a frock coat. The school to which I belong suggests that we should stare steadily at the man until we see the man inside the frock coat. If we stare at him long enough he may even be moved to take off his coat to us; and that is a far greater compliment than his taking off his hat. In other words, we may, by fixing our attention almost fiercely on the facts actually before us, force them to turn into adventures; force them to give up their meaning and fulfil their mysterious purpose. The purpose of the Kipling literature is to show how many extraordinary things a man may see if he is active and strides from continent to continent like the giant in my tale. But the object of my school is to show how many extraordinary things even a lazy and ordinary man may see if he can spur himself to the single activity of seeing. For this purpose I have taken the laziest person of my acquaintance, that is myself; and made an idle diary of such odd things as I have fallen over by accident, in walking in a very limited area at a very indolent pace. If anyone says that these are very small affairs talked about in very big language, I can only gracefully compliment him upon seeing the joke. If anyone says that I am making mountains out of molehills, I confess with pride that it is so. I can imagine no more successful and productive form of manufacture than that of making mountains out of molehills. But I would add this not unimportant fact, that molehills are mountains; one has only to become a pigmy like Peter to discover that.

I have my doubts about all this real value in mountaineering, in getting to the top of everything and overlooking everything. Satan was the most celebrated of Alpine guides, when he took Jesus to the top of an exceeding high mountain and showed him all the kingdoms of the earth. But the joy of Satan in standing on a peak is not a joy in largeness, but a joy in beholding smallness, in the fact that all men look like insects at his feet. It is from the valley that things look large; it is from the level that things look high; I am a child of the level and have no need of that celebrated Alpine guide. I will lift up my eyes to the hills, from whence cometh my help; but I will not lift up my carcass to the hills, unless it is absolutely necessary. Everything is in an attitude of mind; and at this moment I am in a comfortable attitude. I will sit still and let the marvels and the adventures settle on me like flies. There are plenty of them, I assure you. The world will never starve for want of wonders; but only for want of wonder.

II

A Piece of Chalk

I remember one splendid morning, all blue and silver, in the summer holidays when I reluctantly tore myself away from the task of doing nothing in particular, and put on a hat of some sort and picked up a walking-stick, and put six very bright-coloured chalks in my pocket. I then went into the kitchen (which, along with the rest of the house, belonged to a very square and sensible old woman in a Sussex village), and asked the owner and occupant of the kitchen if she had any brown paper. She had a great deal; in fact, she had too much; and she mistook the purpose and the rationale of the existence of brown paper. She seemed to have an idea that if a person wanted brown paper he must be wanting to tie up parcels; which was the last thing I wanted to do; indeed, it is a thing which I have found to be beyond my mental capacity. Hence she dwelt very much on the varying qualities of toughness and endurance in the material. I explained to her that I only wanted to draw pictures on it, and that I did not want them to endure in the least; and that from my point of view, therefore, it was a question, not of tough consistency, but of responsive surface, a thing comparatively irrelevant in a parcel. When she understood that I wanted to draw she offered to overwhelm me with note-paper, apparently supposing that I did my notes and correspondence on old brown paper wrappers from motives of economy.

I then tried to explain the rather delicate logical shade, that I not only liked brown paper, but liked the quality of brownness in paper, just as I liked the quality of brownness in October woods, or in beer, or in the peat-streams of the North. Brown paper represents the primal twilight of the first toil of creation, and with a bright-coloured chalk or two you can pick out points of fire in it, sparks of gold, and blood-red, and sea-green, like the first fierce stars that sprang out of divine darkness. All this I said (in an off-hand way) to the old woman; and I put the brown paper in my pocket along with the chalks, and possibly other things. I suppose every one must have reflected how primeval and how poetical are the things that one carries in one's pocket; the pocket-knife, for instance, the type of all human tools, the infant of the sword.

Once I planned to write a book of poems entirely about the things in my pockets. But I found it would be too long; and the age of the great epics is past.

WITH MY STICK AND MY knife, my chalks and my brown paper, I went out on to the great downs. I crawled across those colossal contours that express the best quality of England, because they are at the same time soft and strong. The smoothness of them has the same meaning as the smoothness of great cart-horses, or the smoothness of the beech-tree; it declares in the teeth of our timid and cruel theories that the mighty are merciful. As my eye swept the landscape, the landscape was as kindly as any of its cottages, but for power it was like an earthquake. The villages in the immense valley were safe, one could see, for centuries; yet the lifting of the whole land was like the lifting of one enormous wave to wash them all away.

I crossed one swell of living turf after another, looking for a place to sit down and draw. Do not, for heaven's sake, imagine I was going to sketch from Nature. I was going to draw devils and seraphim, and blind old gods that men worshipped before the dawn of right, and saints in robes of angry crimson, and seas of strange green, and all the sacred or monstrous symbols that look so well in bright colours on brown paper. They are much better worth drawing than Nature; also they are much easier to draw. When a cow came slouching by in the field next to me, a mere artist might have drawn it; but I always get wrong in the hind legs of quadrupeds. So I drew the soul of the cow; which I saw there plainly walking before me in the sunlight; and the soul was all purple and silver, and had seven horns and the mystery that belongs to all the beasts. But though I could not with a crayon get the best out of the landscape, it does not follow that the landscape was not getting the best out of me. And this, I think, is the mistake that people make about the old poets who lived before Wordsworth, and were supposed not to care very much about Nature because they did not describe it much.

They preferred writing about great men to writing about great hills; but they sat on the great hills to write it. They gave out much less about Nature, but they drank in, perhaps, much more. They painted the white robes of their holy virgins with the blinding snow, at which they had stared all day. They blazoned the shields of their paladins with the purple and gold of many heraldic sunsets. The greenness of a thousand green leaves clustered into the live green figure of Robin Hood. The blueness of a score of forgotten skies became the blue robes of the Virgin. The inspiration went in like sunbeams and came out like Apollo.

But as I sat scrawling these silly figures on the brown paper, it began to dawn on me, to my great disgust, that I had left one chalk, and that a most exquisite and essential chalk, behind. I searched all my pockets, but I could not find any white chalk. Now, those who are acquainted with all the philosophy (nay, religion) which is typified in the art of drawing on brown paper, know that white is positive and essential. I cannot avoid remarking here upon a moral significance. One of the wise and awful truths which this brown-paper art reveals, is this, that white is a colour. It is not a mere absence of colour; it is a shining and affirmative thing, as fierce as red, as definite as black. When, so to speak, your pencil grows red-hot, it draws roses; when it grows white-hot, it draws stars. And one of the two or three defiant verities of the best religious morality, of real Christianity, for example, is exactly this same thing; the chief assertion of religious morality is that white is a colour. Virtue is not the absence of vices or the avoidance of moral dangers; virtue is a vivid and separate thing, like pain or a particular smell. Mercy does not mean not being cruel or sparing people revenge or punishment; it means a plain and positive thing like the sun, which one has either seen or not seen.

Chastity does not mean abstention from sexual wrong; it means something flaming, like Joan of Arc. In a word, God paints in many colours; but He never paints so gorgeously, I had almost said so gaudily, as when He paints in white. In a sense our age has realised this fact, and expressed it in our sullen costume. For if it were really true that white was a blank and colourless thing, negative and non-committal, then white would be used instead of black and grey for the funeral dress of this pessimistic period. We should see city gentlemen in frock coats of spotless silver linen, with top hats as white as wonderful arum lilies. Which is not the case.

Meanwhile, I could not find my chalk.

I sat on the hill in a sort of despair. There was no town nearer than Chichester at which it was even remotely probable that there would be such a thing as an artist's colourman. And yet, without white, my absurd little pictures would be as pointless as the world would be if there were no good people in it. I stared stupidly round, racking my brain for expedients. Then I suddenly stood up and roared with laughter, again and again, so that the cows stared at me and called a committee. Imagine a man in the Sahara regretting that he had no sand for his hour-glass. Imagine a gentleman in mid-ocean wishing that he had brought some salt water with him for his chemical experiments. I was sitting on an immense warehouse of white chalk. The landscape was made entirely out of white chalk. White chalk was piled more miles until it met the sky. I stooped and broke a piece off the rock I sat on; it did not mark so well as the shop chalks do; but it gave the effect. And I stood there in a trance of pleasure, realising that this Southern England is not only a grand peninsula, and a tradition and a civilisation; it is something even more admirable. It is a piece of chalk.

III

The Secret of a Train

All this talk of a railway mystery has sent my mind back to a loose memory. I will not merely say that this story is true: because, as you will soon see, it is all truth and no story. It has no explanation and no conclusion; it is, like most of the other things we encounter in life, a fragment of something else which would be intensely exciting if it were not too large to be seen. For the perplexity of life arises from there being too many interesting things in it for us to be interested properly in any of them; what we call its triviality is really the tag-ends of numberless tales; ordinary and unmeaning existence is like ten thousand thrilling detective stories mixed up with a spoon. My experience was a fragment of this nature, and it is, at any rate, not fictitious. Not only am I not making up the incidents (what there were of them), but I am not making up the atmosphere of the landscape, which were the whole horror of the thing. I remember them vividly, and they were as I shall now describe.

About noon of an ashen autumn day some years ago I was standing outside the station at Oxford intending to take the train to London. And for some reason, out of idleness or the emptiness of my mind or the emptiness of the pale grey sky, or the cold, a kind of caprice fell upon me that I would not go by that train at all, but would step out on the road and walk at least some part of the way to London. I do not know if other people are made like me in this matter; but to me it is always dreary weather, what may be called useless weather, that slings into life a sense of action and romance. On bright blue days I do not want anything to happen; the world is complete and beautiful, a thing for contemplation. I no more ask for adventures under that turquoise dome than I ask for adventures in church. But when the background of man's life is a grey background, then, in the name of man's sacred supremacy, I desire to paint on it in fire and gore. When the heavens fail man refuses to fail; when the sky seems to have written on it, in letters of lead and pale silver, the decree that nothing shall happen, then the immortal soul, the prince of the creatures, rises up and decrees that something shall happen, if it be only the slaughter of a policeman. But this is a digressive way of stating what I have said already—that the bleak sky awoke in me a hunger for some change of plans, that the monotonous weather seemed to render unbearable the use of the monotonous train, and that I set out into the country lanes, out of the town of Oxford. It was, perhaps, at that moment that a strange curse came upon me out of the city and the sky, whereby it was decreed that years afterwards I should, in an article in the DAILY NEWS, talk about Sir George Trevelyan in connection with Oxford, when I knew perfectly well that he went to Cambridge.

As I crossed the country everything was ghostly and colourless. The fields that should have been green were as grey as the skies; the tree-tops that should have been green were as grey as the clouds and as cloudy. And when I had walked for some hours the evening was closing in. A sickly sunset clung weakly to the horizon, as if pale with reluctance to leave the world in the dark. And as it faded more and more the skies seemed to come closer and to threaten. The clouds which had been merely sullen became swollen; and then they loosened and let down the dark curtains of the rain. The rain was blinding and seemed to beat like blows from an enemy at close quarters; the skies seemed bending over and bawling in my ears. I walked on many more miles before I met a man, and in that distance my mind had been made up; and when I met him I asked him if anywhere in the neighbourhood I could pick up the train for Paddington. He directed me to a small silent station (I cannot even remember the name of it) which stood well away from the road and looked as lonely as a hut on the Andes. I do not think I have ever seen such a type of time and sadness and scepticism and everything devilish as that station was: it looked as if it had always been raining there ever since the creation of the world. The water streamed from the soaking wood of it as if it were not water at all, but some loathsome liquid corruption of the wood itself; as if the solid station were eternally falling to pieces and pouring away in filth. It took me nearly ten minutes to find a man in the station. When I did he was a dull one, and when I asked him if there was a train to Paddington his answer was sleepy and vague. As far as I understood him, he said there would be a train in half an hour. I sat down and lit a cigar and waited, watching the last tail of the tattered sunset and listening to the everlasting rain. It may have been in half an hour or less, but a train came rather slowly into the station.

It was an unnaturally dark train; I could not see a light anywhere in the long black body of it; and I could not see any guard running beside it. I was reduced to walking up to the engine and calling out to the stoker to ask if the train was going to London. "Well—yes, sir," he said, with an unaccountable kind of reluctance. "It is going to London; but—" It was just starting, and I jumped into the first carriage; it was pitch dark. I sat there smoking and wondering, as we steamed through the continually darkening landscape, lined with desolate poplars, until we slowed down and stopped, irrationally, in the middle of a field. I heard a heavy noise as of some one clambering off the train, and a dark, ragged head suddenly put itself into my window. "Excuse me, sir," said the stoker, "but I think, perhaps—well, perhaps you ought to know—there's a dead man in this train."

HAD I BEEN A TRUE artist, a person of exquisite susceptibilities and nothing else, I should have been bound, no doubt, to be finally overwhelmed with this sensational touch, and to have insisted on getting out and walking. As it was, I regret to say, I expressed myself politely, but firmly, to the effect that I didn't care particularly if the train took me to Paddington. But when the train had started with its unknown burden I did do one thing, and do it quite instinctively, without stopping to think, or to think more than a flash. I threw away my cigar. Something that is as old as man and has to do with all mourning and ceremonial told me to do it. There was something unnecessarily horrible, it seemed to me, in the idea of there being only two men in that train, and one of them dead and the other smoking a cigar. And as the red and gold of the butt end of it faded like a funeral torch trampled out at some symbolic moment of a procession, I realised how immortal ritual is. I realised (what is the origin and essence of all ritual) that in the presence of those sacred riddles about which we can say nothing it is more decent merely to do something. And I realised that ritual will always mean throwing away something; DESTROYING our corn or wine upon the altar of our gods.

When the train panted at last into Paddington Station I sprang out of it with a suddenly released curiosity. There was a barrier and officials guarding the rear part of the train; no one was allowed to press towards it. They were guarding and hiding something; perhaps death in some too shocking form, perhaps something like the Merstham matter, so mixed up with human mystery and wickedness that the land has to

G.K. CHESTERTON

give it a sort of sanctity; perhaps something worse than either. I went out gladly enough into the streets and saw the lamps shining on the laughing faces. Nor have I ever known from that day to this into what strange story I wandered or what frightful thing was my companion in the dark.

IV

The Perfect Game

We have all met the man who says that some odd things have happened to him, but that he does not really believe that they were supernatural. My own position is the opposite of this. I believe in the supernatural as a matter of intellect and reason, not as a matter of personal experience. I do not see ghosts; I only see their inherent probability. But it is entirely a matter of the mere intelligence, not even of the motions; my nerves and body are altogether of this earth, very earthy. But upon people of this temperament one weird incident will often leave a peculiar impression. And the weirdest circumstance that ever occurred to me occurred a little while ago. It consisted in nothing less than my playing a game, and playing it quite well for some seventeen consecutive minutes. The ghost of my grandfather would have astonished me less.

On one of these blue and burning afternoons I found myself, to my inexpressible astonishment, playing a game called croquet. I had imagined that it belonged to the epoch of Leach and Anthony Trollope, and I had neglected to provide myself with those very long and luxuriant side whiskers which are really essential to such a scene. I played it with a man whom we will call Parkinson, and with whom I had a semi-philosophical argument which lasted through the entire contest. It is deeply implanted in my mind that I had the best of the argument; but it is certain and beyond dispute that I had the worst of the game.

"Oh, Parkinson, Parkinson!" I cried, patting him affectionately on the head with a mallet, "how far you really are from the pure love of the sport—you who can play. It is only we who play badly who love the Game itself. You love glory; you love applause; you love the earthquake voice of victory; you do not love croquet. You do not love croquet until you love being beaten at croquet. It is we the bunglers who adore the occupation in the abstract. It is we to whom it is art for art's sake. If we may see the face of Croquet herself (if I may so express myself) we are content to see her face turned upon us in anger. Our play is called amateurish; and we wear proudly the name of amateur, for amateurs is but the French for Lovers. We accept all adventures from our Lady, the most disastrous or the most dreary. We wait outside her iron gates (I allude to the hoops), vainly essaying to enter. Our devoted balls, impetuous and full of chivalry, will not be confined within the pedantic boundaries of the mere croquet ground. Our balls seek honour in the ends of the earth; they turn up in the flower-beds and the conservatory; they are to be found in the front garden and the next street. No, Parkinson! The good painter has skill. It is the bad painter who loves his art. The good musician loves being a musician, the bad musician loves music. With such a pure and hopeless passion do I worship croquet. I love the game itself. I love the parallelogram of grass marked out with chalk or tape, as if its limits were the frontiers of my sacred Fatherland, the four seas of Britain. I love the mere swing of the mallets, and the click of the balls is music. The four colours are to me sacramental and symbolic, like the red of martyrdom, or the white of Easter Day. You lose all this, my poor Parkinson. You have to solace yourself for the absence of this vision by the paltry consolation of being able to go through hoops and to hit the stick."

And I waved my mallet in the air with a graceful gaiety.

"Don't be too sorry for me," said Parkinson, with his simple sarcasm. "I shall get over it in time. But it seems to me that the more a man likes a game the better he would want to play it. Granted that the pleasure in the thing itself comes first, does not the pleasure of success come naturally and inevitably afterwards? Or, take your own simile of the Knight and his Lady-love. I admit the gentleman does first and foremost want to be in the lady's presence. But I never yet heard of a gentleman who wanted to look an utter ass when he was there."

"Perhaps not; though he generally looks it," I replied. "But the truth is that there is a fallacy in the simile, although it was my own. The happiness at which the lover is aiming is an infinite happiness, which can be extended without limit. The more he is loved, normally speaking, the jollier he will be. It is definitely true that the stronger the love of both lovers, the stronger will be the happiness. But it is not true that the stronger the play of both croquet players the stronger will be the game. It is logically possible—(follow me closely here, Parkinson!)—it is logically possible, to play croquet too well to enjoy it at all. If you could put this blue ball through that distant hoop as easily as you could pick it up with your hand, then you would not put it through that hoop any more than you pick it up with your hand; it would not be worth doing.

If you could play unerringly you would not play at all. The moment the game is perfect the game disappears."

"I do not think, however," said Parkinson, "that you are in any immediate danger of effecting that sort of destruction. I do not think your croquet will vanish through its own faultless excellence. You are safe for the present."

I again caressed him with the mallet, knocked a ball about, wired myself, and resumed the thread of my discourse.

The long, warm evening had been gradually closing in, and by this time it was almost twilight. By the time I had delivered four more fundamental principles, and my companion had gone through five more hoops, the dusk was verging upon dark.

"We shall have to give this up," said Parkinson, as he missed a ball almost for the first time, "I can't see a thing."

"Nor can I," I answered, "and it is a comfort to reflect that I could not hit anything if I saw it."

With that I struck a ball smartly, and sent it away into the darkness towards where the shadowy figure of Parkinson moved in the hot haze. Parkinson immediately uttered a loud and dramatic cry. The situation, indeed, called for it. I had hit the right ball.

Stunned with astonishment, I crossed the gloomy ground, and hit my ball again. It went through a hoop. I could not see the hoop; but it was the right hoop. I shuddered from head to foot.

Words were wholly inadequate, so I slouched heavily after that impossible ball. Again I hit it away into the night, in what I supposed was the vague direction of the quite invisible stick. And in the dead silence I heard the stick rattle as the ball struck it heavily.

I threw down my mallet. "I can't stand this," I said. "My ball has gone right three times. These things are not of this world."

"Pick your mallet up," said Parkinson, "have another go."

"I tell you I daren't. If I made another hoop like that I should see all the devils dancing there on the blessed grass."

"Why devils?" asked Parkinson; "they may be only fairies making fun of you. They are sending you the 'Perfect Game,' which is no game."

I looked about me. The garden was full of a burning darkness, in which the faint glimmers had the look of fire. I stepped across the grass as if it burnt me, picked up the mallet, and hit the ball somewhere— somewhere where another ball might be. I heard the dull click of the balls touching, and ran into the house like one pursued.

G.K. CHESTERTON

V

The Extraordinary Cabman

From time to time I have introduced into this newspaper column the narration of incidents that have really occurred. I do not mean to insinuate that in this respect it stands alone among newspaper columns. I mean only that I have found that my meaning was better expressed by some practical parable out of daily life than by any other method; therefore I propose to narrate the incident of the extraordinary cabman, which occurred to me only three days ago, and which, slight as it apparently is, aroused in me a moment of genuine emotion bordering upon despair.

On the day that I met the strange cabman I had been lunching in a little restaurant in Soho in company with three or four of my best friends. My best friends are all either bottomless sceptics or quite uncontrollable believers, so our discussion at luncheon turned upon the most ultimate and terrible ideas. And the whole argument worked out ultimately to this: that the question is whether a man can be certain of anything at all. I think he can be certain, for if (as I said to my friend, furiously brandishing an empty bottle) it is impossible intellectually to entertain certainty, what is this certainty which it is impossible to entertain? If I have never experienced such a thing as certainty I cannot even say that a thing is not certain. Similarly, if I have never experienced such a thing as green I cannot even say that my nose is not green. It may be as green as possible for all I know, if I have really no experience of greenness. So we shouted at each other and shook the room; because metaphysics is the only thoroughly emotional thing. And the difference between us was very deep, because it was a difference as to the object of the whole thing called broad-mindedness or the opening of the intellect. For my friend said that he opened his intellect as the sun opens the fans of a palm tree, opening for opening's sake, opening infinitely for ever. But I said that I opened my intellect as I opened my mouth, in order to shut it again on something solid. I was doing it at the moment. And as I truly pointed out, it would look uncommonly silly if I went on opening my mouth infinitely, for ever and ever.

NOW WHEN THIS ARGUMENT WAS over, or at least when it was cut short (for it will never be over), I went away with one of my companions, who in the confusion and comparative insanity of a General Election had somehow become a member of Parliament, and I drove with him in a cab from the corner of Leicester-square to the members' entrance of the House of Commons, where the police received me with a quite unusual tolerance. Whether they thought that he was my keeper or that I was his keeper is a discussion between us which still continues.

It is necessary in this narrative to preserve the utmost exactitude of detail. After leaving my friend at the House I took the cab on a few hundred yards to an office in Victoria-street which I had to visit. I then got out and offered him more than his fare. He looked at it, but not with the surly doubt and general disposition to try it on which is not unknown among normal cabmen. But this was no normal, perhaps, no human, cabman. He looked at it with a dull and infantile astonishment, clearly quite genuine. "Do you know, sir," he said, "you've only given me 1s.8d?" I remarked, with some surprise, that I did know it. "Now you know, sir," said he in a kindly, appealing, reasonable way, "you know that ain't the fare from Euston." "Euston," I repeated vaguely, for the phrase at that moment sounded to me like China or Arabia. "What on earth has Euston got to do with it?" "You hailed me just outside Euston Station," began the man with astonishing precision, "and then you said—" "What in the name of Tartarus are you talking about?" I said with Christian forbearance; "I took you at the south-west corner of Leicester-square." "Leicester-square," he exclaimed, loosening a kind of cataract of scorn, "why we ain't been near Leicester-square to-day. You hailed me outside Euston Station, and you said—" "Are you mad, or am I?" I asked with scientific calm.

I looked at the man. No ordinary dishonest cabman would think of creating so solid and colossal and creative a lie. And this man was not a dishonest cabman. If ever a human face was heavy and simple and humble, and with great big blue eyes protruding like a frog's, if ever (in short) a human face was all that a human face should be, it was the face of that resentful and respectful cabman. I looked up and down the street; an unusually dark twilight seemed to be coming on. And for one second the old nightmare of the sceptic put its finger on my nerve. What was certainty? Was anybody certain of anything? Heavens! to think of the dull rut of the sceptics who go on asking whether we possess a future life. The exciting question for real scepticism is whether we possess a past life. What is a minute ago, rationalistically considered, except a tradition and a picture? The darkness grew deeper from the road. The cabman calmly gave me the most elaborate details of the gesture, the words, the complex but consistent course of action which I had adopted since that remarkable occasion when I had hailed him outside Euston Station. How did I know (my sceptical friends would say) that I had not hailed him outside Euston. I was firm about my assertion; he was quite equally firm about his. He was obviously quite as honest a man as I, and a member of a much more respectable profession. In that moment the universe and the stars swung just a hair's breadth from their balance, and the foundations of the earth were moved. But for the same reason that I believe in Democracy, for the same reason that I believe in free will, for the same reason that I believe in fixed character of virtue, the reason that could only be expressed by saying that I do not choose to be a lunatic, I continued to believe that this honest cabman was wrong, and I repeated to him that I had really taken him at the corner of Leicester-square. He began with the same evident and ponderous sincerity, "You hailed me outside Euston Station, and you said—"

And at this moment there came over his features a kind of frightful transfiguration of living astonishment, as if he had been lit up like a lamp from the inside. "Why, I beg your pardon, sir," he said. "I beg your pardon. I beg your pardon. You took me from Leicester-square. I remember now. I beg your pardon." And with that this astonishing man let out his whip with a sharp crack at his horse and went trundling away. The whole of which interview, before the banner of St. George I swear, is strictly true.

I LOOKED AT THE STRANGE cabman as he lessened in the distance and the mists. I do not know whether I was right in fancying that although his face had seemed so honest there was something unearthly and demoniac about him when seen from behind. Perhaps he had been sent to tempt me from my adherence to those sanities and certainties which I had defended earlier in the day. In any case it gave me pleasure to remember that my sense of reality, though it had rocked for an instant, had remained erect.

VI

AN ACCIDENT

Some time ago I wrote in these columns an article called "The Extraordinary Cabman." I am now in a position to contribute my experience of a still more extraordinary cab. The extraordinary thing about the cab was that it did not like me; it threw me out violently in the middle of the Strand. If my friends who read the DAILY NEWS are as romantic (and as rich) as I take them to be, I presume that this experience is not uncommon. I suppose that they are all being thrown out of cabs, all over London. Still, as there are some people, virginal and remote from the world, who have not yet had this luxurious experience, I will give a short account of the psychology of myself when my hansom cab ran into the side of a motor omnibus, and I hope hurt it.

I do not need to dwell on the essential romance of the hansom cab—that one really noble modern thing which our age, when it is judged, will gravely put beside the Parthenon. It is really modern in that it is both secret and swift. My particular hansom cab was modern in these two respects; it was also very modern in the fact that it came to grief. But it is also English; it is not to be found abroad; it belongs to a beautiful, romantic country where nearly everybody is pretending to be richer than they are, and acting as if they were. It is comfortable, and yet it is reckless; and that combination is the very soul of England. But although I had always realised all these good qualities in a hansom cab, I had not experienced all the possibilities, or, as the moderns put it, all the aspects of that vehicle. My enunciation of the merits of a hansom cab had been always made when it was the right way up. Let me, therefore, explain how I felt when I fell out of a hansom cab for the first and, I am happy to believe, the last time. Polycrates threw one ring into the sea to propitiate the Fates. I have thrown one hansom cab into the sea (if you will excuse a rather violent metaphor) and the Fates are, I am quite sure, propitiated. Though I am told they do not like to be told so.

I was driving yesterday afternoon in a hansom cab down one of the sloping streets into the Strand, reading one of my own admirable articles with continual pleasure, and still more continual surprise, when the horse fell forward, scrambled a moment on the scraping stones, staggered to his feet again, and went forward. The horses in my cabs often do this, and I have learnt to enjoy my own articles at any angle of the vehicle. So I did not see anything at all odd about the way the horse went on again. But I saw it suddenly in the faces of all the people on the pavement. They were all turned towards me, and they were all struck with fear suddenly, as with a white flame out of the sky. And one man half ran out into the road with a movement of the elbow as if warding off a blow, and tried to stop the horse. Then I knew that the reins were lost, and the next moment the horse was like a living thunder-bolt. I try to describe things exactly as they seemed to me; many details I may have missed or mis-stated; many details may have, so to speak, gone mad in the race down the road. I remember that I once called one of my experiences narrated in this paper "A Fragment of Fact." This is, at any rate, a fragment of fact. No fact could possibly be more fragmentary than the sort of fact that I expected to be at the bottom of that street.

I BELIEVE IN PREACHING TO the converted; for I have generally found that the converted do not understand their own religion. Thus I have always urged in this paper that democracy has a deeper meaning than democrats understand; that is, that common and popular things, proverbs, and ordinary sayings always have something in them unrealised by most who repeat them. Here is one. We have all heard about the man who is in momentary danger, and who sees the whole of his life pass before him in a moment. In the cold, literal, and common sense of words, this is obviously a thundering lie. Nobody can pretend that in an accident or a mortal crisis he elaborately remembered all the tickets he had ever taken to Wimbledon, or all the times that he had ever passed the brown bread and butter.

But in those few moments, while my cab was tearing towards the traffic of the Strand, I discovered that there is a truth behind this phrase, as there is behind all popular phrases. I did really have, in that short and shrieking period, a rapid succession of a number of fundamental points of view. I had, so to speak, about five religions in almost as many seconds. My first religion was pure Paganism, which among sincere men is more shortly described as extreme fear. Then there succeeded a state of mind which is quite real, but for which no proper name has ever been found. The ancients called it Stoicism, and I think it must be what some German lunatics mean (if they mean anything) when they talk about Pessimism. It was an empty and open acceptance of the thing that happens—as if one had got beyond the value of it. And then, curiously enough, came a very strong contrary feeling—that things mattered very much indeed, and yet that they were something more than tragic. It was a feeling, not that life was unimportant, but that life was much too important ever to be anything but life. I hope that this was Christianity. At any rate, it occurred at the moment when we went crash into the omnibus.

It seemed to me that the hansom cab simply turned over on top of me, like an enormous hood or hat. I then found myself crawling out from underneath it in attitudes so undignified that they must have added enormously to that great cause to which the Anti-Puritan League and I have recently dedicated ourselves. I mean the cause of the pleasures of the people. As to my demeanour when I emerged, I have two confessions to make, and they are both made merely in the interests of mental science. The first is that whereas I had been in a quite pious frame of mind the moment before the collision, when I got to my feet and found I had got off with a cut or two I began (like St. Peter) to curse and to swear. A man offered me a newspaper or something that I had dropped. I can distinctly remember consigning the paper to a state of irremediable spiritual ruin. I am very sorry for this now, and I apologise both to the man and to the paper. I have not the least idea what was the meaning of this unnatural anger; I mention it as a psychological confession. It was immediately followed by extreme hilarity, and I made so many silly jokes to the policeman that he disgraced himself by continual laughter before all the little boys in the street, who had hitherto taken him seriously.

THERE IS ONE OTHER ODD thing about the matter which I also mention as a curiosity of the human brain or deficiency of brain. At intervals of about every three minutes I kept on reminding the policeman that I had not paid the cabman, and that I hoped he would not lose his money. He said it would be all right, and the man would appear. But it was not until about half an hour afterwards that it suddenly struck me with a shock intolerable that the man might conceivably have lost more than half a crown; that he had been in danger as well as I. I had instinctively regarded the cabman as something uplifted above accidents, a god. I immediately made inquiries, and I am happy to say that they seemed to have been unnecessary.

But henceforward I shall always understand with a darker and more delicate charity those who take tythe of mint, and anise, and cumin, and neglect the weightier matters of the law; I shall remember how I was once really tortured with owing half a crown to a man who might have been dead. Some admirable men in white coats at the Charing Cross Hospital tied up my small injury, and I went out again into the Strand. I felt upon me even a kind of unnatural youth; I hungered for something untried. So to open a new chapter in my life I got into a hansom cab.

VII

The Advantages of Having One Leg

A friend of mine who was visiting a poor woman in bereavement and casting about for some phrase of consolation that should not be either insolent or weak, said at last, "I think one can live through these great sorrows and even be the better. What wears one is the little worries." "That's quite right, mum," answered the old woman with emphasis, "and I ought to know, seeing I've had ten of 'em." It is, perhaps, in this sense that it is most true that little worries are most wearing. In its vaguer significance the phrase, though it contains a truth, contains also some possibilities of self-deception and error. People who have both small troubles and big ones have the right to say that they find the small ones the most bitter; and it is undoubtedly true that the back which is bowed under loads incredible can feel a faint addition to those loads; a giant holding up the earth and all its animal creation might still find the grasshopper a burden. But I am afraid that the maxim that the smallest worries are the worst is sometimes used or abused by people, because they have nothing but the very smallest worries. The lady may excuse herself for reviling the crumpled rose leaf by reflecting with what extraordinary dignity she would wear the crown of thorns—if she had to. The gentleman may permit himself to curse the dinner and tell himself that he would behave much better if it were a mere matter of starvation. We need not deny that the grasshopper on man's shoulder is a burden; but we need not pay much respect to the gentleman who is always calling out that he would rather have an elephant when he knows there are no elephants in the country. We may concede that a straw may break the camel's back, but we like to know that it really is the last straw and not the first.

I grant that those who have serious wrongs have a real right to grumble, so long as they grumble about something else. It is a singular fact that if they are sane they almost always do grumble about something else. To talk quite reasonably about your own quite real wrongs is the quickest way to go off your head. But people with great troubles talk about little ones, and the man who complains of the crumpled rose leaf very often has his flesh full of the thorns. But if a man has commonly a very clear and happy daily life then I think we are justified in asking that he shall not make mountains out of molehills. I do no deny that molehills can sometimes be important. Small annoyances have this evil about them, that they can be more abrupt because they are more invisible; they cast no shadow before, they have no atmosphere. No one ever had a mystical premonition that he was going to tumble over a hassock. William III died by falling over a molehill; I do not suppose that with all his varied abilities he could have managed to fall over a mountain. But when all this is allowed for, I repeat that we may ask a happy man (not William III) to put up with pure inconveniences, and even make them part of his happiness. Of positive pain or positive poverty I do not here speak. I speak of those innumerable accidental limitations that are always falling across our path—bad weather, confinement to this or that house or room, failure of appointments or arrangements, waiting at railway stations, missing posts, finding unpunctuality when we want punctuality, or, what is worse, finding punctuality when we don't. It is of the poetic pleasures to be drawn from all these that I sing—I sing with confidence because I have recently been experimenting in the poetic pleasures which arise from having to sit in one chair with a sprained foot, with the only alternative course of standing on one leg like a stork—a stork is a poetic simile; therefore I eagerly adopted it.

To appreciate anything we must always isolate it, even if the thing itself symbolise something other than isolation. If we wish to see what a house is it must be a house in some uninhabited landscape. If we wish to depict what a man really is we must depict a man alone in a desert or on a dark sea sand. So long as he is a single figure he means all that humanity means; so long as he is solitary he means human society; so long as he is solitary he means sociability and comradeship. Add another figure and the picture is less human—not more so. One is company, two is none. If you wish to symbolise human building draw one dark tower on the horizon; if you wish to symbolise light let there be no star in the sky. Indeed, all through that strangely lit season which we call our day there is but one star in the sky—a large, fierce star which we call the sun. One sun is splendid; six suns would be only vulgar. One Tower Of Giotto is sublime; a row of Towers of Giotto would be only like a row of white posts. The poetry of art is in beholding the single tower; the poetry of nature in seeing the single tree; the poetry of love in following the single woman; the poetry of religion in worshipping the single star. And so, in the same pensive lucidity, I find the poetry of all human anatomy in standing on a single leg. To express complete and perfect leggishness the leg must stand in sublime isolation, like the tower in the wilderness. As Ibsen so finely says, the strongest leg is that which stands most alone.

This lonely leg on which I rest has all the simplicity of some Doric column. The students of architecture tell us that the only legitimate use of a column is to support weight. This column of mine fulfils its legitimate function. It supports weight. Being of an animal and organic consistency, it may even improve by the process, and during these few days that I am thus unequally balanced, the helplessness or dislocation of the one leg may find compensation in the astonishing strength and classic beauty of the other leg. Mrs. Mountstuart Jenkinson in Mr. George Meredith's novel might pass by at any moment, and seeing me in the stork-like attitude would exclaim, with equal admiration and a more literal exactitude, "He has a leg." Notice how this famous literary phrase supports my contention touching this isolation of any admirable thing. Mrs. Mountstuart Jenkinson, wishing to make a clear and perfect picture of human grace, said that Sir Willoughby Patterne had a leg. She delicately glossed over and concealed the clumsy and offensive fact that he had really two legs. Two legs were superfluous and irrelevant, a reflection, and a confusion. Two legs would have confused Mrs. Mountstuart Jenkinson like two Monuments in London. That having had one good leg he should have another—this would be to use vain repetitions as the Gentiles do. She would have been as much bewildered by him as if he had been a centipede.

All pessimism has a secret optimism for its object. All surrender of life, all denial of pleasure, all darkness, all austerity, all desolation has for its real aim this separation of something so that it may be poignantly and perfectly enjoyed. I feel grateful for the slight sprain which has introduced this mysterious and fascinating division between one of my feet and the other. The way to love anything is to realise that it might be lost. In one of my feet I can feel how strong and splendid a foot is; in the other I can realise how very much otherwise it might have been. The moral of the thing is wholly exhilarating. This world and all our powers in it are far more awful and beautiful than even we know until some accident reminds us. If you wish to perceive that limitless felicity, limit yourself if only for a moment. If you wish to realise how fearfully and wonderfully God's image is made, stand on one leg. If you want to realise the splendid vision of all visible things—wink the other eye.

VIII

The End of the World

For some time I had been wandering in quiet streets in the curious town of Besançon, which stands like a sort of peninsula in a horse-shoe of river. You may learn from the guide books that it was the birthplace of Victor Hugo, and that it is a military station with many forts, near the French frontier. But you will not learn from guide books that the very tiles on the roofs seem to be of some quainter and more delicate colour than the tiles of all the other towns of the world; that the tiles look like the little clouds of some strange sunset, or like the lustrous scales of some strange fish. They will not tell you that in this town the eye cannot rest on anything without finding it in some way attractive and even elvish, a carved face at a street corner, a gleam of green fields through a stunted arch, or some unexpected colour for the enamel of a spire or dome.

Evening was coming on and in the light of it all these colours so simple and yet so subtle seemed more and more to fit together and make a fairy tale. I sat down for a little outside a café with a row of little toy trees in front of it, and presently the driver of a fly (as we should call it) came to the same place. He was one of those very large and dark Frenchmen, a type not common but yet typical of France; the Rabelaisian Frenchman, huge, swarthy, purple-faced, a walking wine-barrel; he was a sort of Southern Falstaff, if one can imagine Falstaff anything but English. And, indeed, there was a vital difference, typical of two nations. For while Falstaff would have been shaking with hilarity like a huge jelly, full of the broad farce of the London streets, this Frenchman was rather solemn and dignified than otherwise—as if pleasure were a kind of pagan religion. After some talk which was full of the admirable civility and equality of French civilisation, he suggested without either eagerness or embarrassment that he should take me in his fly for an hour's ride in the hills beyond the town. And though it was growing late I consented; for there was one long white road under an archway and round a hill that dragged me like a long white cord. We drove through the strong, squat gateway that was made by Romans, and I remember the coincidence like a sort of omen that as we passed out of the city I heard simultaneously the three sounds which are the trinity of France. They make what some poet calls "a tangled trinity," and I am not going to disentangle it. Whatever those three things mean, how or why they co-exist; whether they can be reconciled or perhaps are reconciled already; the three sounds I heard then by an accident all at once make up the French mystery. For the brass band in the Casino gardens behind me was playing with a sort of passionate levity some ramping tune from a Parisian comic opera, and while this was going on I heard also the bugles on the hills above, that told of terrible loyalties and men always arming in the gate of France; and I heard also, fainter than these sounds and through them all, the Angelus.

AFTER THIS COINCIDENCE OF SYMBOLS I had a curious sense of having left France behind me, or, perhaps, even the civilised world. And, indeed, there was something in the landscape wild enough to encourage such a fancy. I have seen perhaps higher mountains, but I have never seen higher rocks; I have never seen height so near, so abrupt and sensational, splinters of rock that stood up like the spires of churches, cliffs that fell sudden and straight as Satan fell from heaven. There was also a quality in the ride which was not only astonishing, but rather bewildering; a quality which many must have noticed if they have driven or ridden rapidly up mountain roads. I mean a sense of gigantic gyration, as of the whole earth turning about one's head. It is quite inadequate to say that the hills rose and fell like enormous waves. Rather the hills seemed to turn about me like the enormous sails of a windmill, a vast wheel of monstrous archangelic wings. As we drove on and up into the gathering purple of the sunset this dizziness increased, confounding things above with things below. Wide walls of wooded rock stood out above my head like a roof. I stared at them until I fancied that I was staring down at a wooded plain. Below me steeps of green swept down to the river. I stared at them until I fancied that they swept up to the sky. The purple darkened, night drew nearer; it seemed only to cut clearer the chasms and draw higher the spires of that nightmare landscape. Above me in the twilight was the huge black hulk of the driver, and his broad, blank back was as mysterious as the back of Death in Watts' picture. I felt that I was growing too fantastic, and I sought to speak of ordinary things. I called out to the driver in French, "Where are you taking me?" and it is a literal and solemn fact that he answered me in the same language without turning around, "To the end of the world."

I did not answer. I let him drag the vehicle up dark, steep ways, until I saw lights under a low roof of little trees and two children, one oddly beautiful, playing at ball. Then we found ourselves filling up the strict main street of a tiny hamlet, and across the wall of its inn was written in large letters, Le Bout Du Monde—the end of the world.

The driver and I sat down outside that inn without a word, as if all ceremonies were natural and understood in that ultimate place. I ordered bread for both of us, and red wine, that was good but had no name. On the other side of the road was a little plain church with a cross on top of it and a cock on top of the cross. This seemed to me a very good end of the world; if the story of the world ended here it ended well. Then I wondered whether I myself should really be content to end here, where most certainly there were the best things of Christendom—a church and children's games and decent soil and a tavern for men to talk with men. But as I thought a singular doubt and desire grew slowly in me, and at last I started up.

"Are you not satisfied?" asked my companion. "No," I said, "I am not satisfied even at the end of the world."

Then, after a silence, I said, "Because you see there are two ends of the world. And this is the wrong end of the world; at least the wrong one for me. This is the French end of the world. I want the other end of the world. Drive me to the other end of the world."

"The other end of the world?" he asked. "Where is that?"

"It is in Walham Green," I whispered hoarsely. "You see it on the London omnibuses. 'World's End and Walham Green.' Oh, I know how good this is; I love your vineyards and your free peasantry, but I want the English end of the world. I love you like a brother, but I want an English cabman, who will be funny and ask me what his fare 'is.' Your bugles stir my blood, but I want to see a London policeman. Take, oh, take me to see a London policeman."

He stood quite dark and still against the end of the sunset, and I could not tell whether he understood or not. I got back into his carriage.

"You will understand," I said, "if ever you are an exile even for pleasure. The child to his mother, the man to his country, as a countryman of yours once said. But since, perhaps, it is rather too long a drive to the English end of the world, we may as well drive back to Besançon."

Only as the stars came out among those immortal hills I wept for Walham Green.

IX

IN THE PLACE DE LA BASTILLE

On the first of May I was sitting outside a café in the Place de la Bastille in Paris staring at the exultant column, crowned with a capering figure, which stands in the place where the people destroyed a prison and ended an age. The thing is a curious example of how symbolic is the great part of human history. As a matter of mere material fact, the Bastille when it was taken was not a horrible prison; it was hardly a prison at all. But it was a symbol, and the people always go by a sure instinct for symbols; for the Chinaman, for instance, at the last General Election, or for President Kruger's hat in the election before; their poetic sense is perfect. The Chinaman with his pigtail is not an idle flippancy. He does typify with a compact precision exactly the thing the people resent in African policy, the alien and grotesque nature of the power of wealth, the fact that money has no roots, that it is not a natural and familiar power, but a sort of airy and evil magic calling monsters from the ends of the earth. The people hate the mine owner who can bring a Chinaman flying across the sea, exactly as the people hated the wizard who could fetch a flying dragon through the air. It was the same with Mr. Kruger's hat. His hat (that admirable hat) was not merely a joke. It did symbolise, and symbolise extremely well, the exact thing which our people at that moment regarded with impatience and venom; the old-fashioned, dingy, Republican simplicity, the unbeautiful dignity of the bourgeois, and the heavier truisms of political morality. No; the people are sometimes wrong on the practical side of politics; they are never wrong on the artistic side.

So it was, certainly, with the Bastille. The destruction of the Bastille was not a reform; it was something more important than a reform. It was an iconoclasm; it was the breaking of a stone image. The people saw the building like a giant looking at them with a score of eyes, and they struck at it as at a carved fact. For of all the shapes in which that immense illusion called materialism can terrify the soul, perhaps the most oppressive are big buildings. Man feels like a fly, an accident, in the thing he has himself made. It requires a violent effort of the spirit to remember that man made this confounding thing and man could unmake it. Therefore the mere act of the ragged people in the street taking and destroying a huge public building has a spiritual, a ritual meaning far beyond its immediate political results. It is a religious service. If, for instance, the Socialists were numerous or courageous enough to capture and smash up the Bank of England, you might argue for ever about the inutility of the act, and how it really did not touch the root of the economic problem in the correct manner. But mankind would never forget it. It would change the world.

Architecture is a very good test of the true strength of a society, for the most valuable things in a human state are the irrevocable things— marriage, for instance. And architecture approaches nearer than any other art to being irrevocable, because it is so difficult to get rid of. You can turn a picture with its face to the wall; it would be a nuisance to turn that Roman cathedral with its face to the wall. You can tear a poem to pieces; it is only in moments of very sincere emotion that you tear a town-hall to pieces. A building is akin to dogma; it is insolent, like a dogma. Whether or no it is permanent, it claims permanence like a dogma. People ask why we have no typical architecture of the modern world, like impressionism in painting. Surely it is obviously because we have not enough dogmas; we cannot bear to see anything in the sky that is solid and enduring, anything in the sky that does not change like the clouds of the sky. But along with this decision which is involved in creating a building, there goes a quite similar decision in the more delightful task of smashing one. The two of necessity go together. In few places have so many fine public buildings been set up as here in Paris, and in few places have so many been destroyed. When people have finally got into the horrible habit of preserving buildings, they have got out of the habit of building them. And in London one mingles, as it were, one's tears because so few are pulled down.

As I sat staring at the column of the Bastille, inscribed to Liberty and Glory, there came out of one corner of the square (which, like so many such squares, was at once crowded and quiet) a sudden and silent line of horsemen. Their dress was of a dull blue, plain and prosaic enough, but the sun set on fire the brass and steel of their helmets; and their helmets were carved like the helmets of the Romans. I had seen them by twos and threes often enough before. I had seen plenty of them in pictures toiling through the snows of Friedland or roaring round the squares at Waterloo. But now they came file after file, like an invasion, and something in their numbers, or in the evening light that lit up their faces and their crests, or something in the reverie into which they broke, made me inclined to spring to my feet and cry out, "The French soldiers!" There were the little men with the brown faces that had so often ridden through the capitals of Europe as coolly as they now rode through their own. And when I looked across the square I saw that the two other corners were choked with blue and red; held by little groups of infantry. The city was garrisoned as against a revolution.

Of course, I had heard all about the strike, chiefly from a baker. He said he was not going to "Chomer." I said, "Qu'est-ce que c'est que le chome?" He said, "Ils ne veulent pas travailler." I said, "Ni moi non plus," and he thought I was a class-conscious collectivist proletarian. The whole thing was curious, and the true moral of it one not easy for us, as a nation, to grasp, because our own faults are so deeply and dangerously in the other direction. To me, as an Englishman (personally steeped in the English optimism and the English dislike of severity), the whole thing seemed a fuss about nothing. It looked like turning out one of the best armies in Europe against ordinary people walking about the street. The cavalry charged us once or twice, more or less harmlessly. But, of course, it is hard to say how far in such criticisms one is assuming the French populace to be (what it is not) as docile as the English. But the deeper truth of the matter tingled, so to speak, through the whole noisy night. This people has a natural faculty for feeling itself on the eve of something—of the Bartholomew or the Revolution or the Commune or the Day of Judgment. It is this sense of crisis that makes France eternally young. It is perpetually pulling down and building up, as it pulled down the prison and put up the column in the Place de La Bastille. France has always been at the point of dissolution. She has found the only method of immortality. She dies daily.

X

On Lying in Bed

Lying in bed would be an altogether perfect and supreme experience if only one had a coloured pencil long enough to draw on the ceiling. This, however, is not generally a part of the domestic apparatus on the premises. I think myself that the thing might be managed with several pails of Aspinall and a broom. Only if one worked in a really sweeping and masterly way, and laid on the colour in great washes, it might drip down again on one's face in floods of rich and mingled colour like some strange fairy rain; and that would have its disadvantages. I am afraid it would be necessary to stick to black and white in this form of artistic composition. To that purpose, indeed, the white ceiling would be of the greatest possible use; in fact, it is the only use I think of a white ceiling being put to.

But for the beautiful experiment of lying in bed I might never have discovered it. For years I have been looking for some blank spaces in a modern house to draw on. Paper is much too small for any really allegorical design; as Cyrano de Bergerac says, "Il me faut des géants." But when I tried to find these fine clear spaces in the modern rooms such as we all live in I was continually disappointed. I found an endless pattern and complication of small objects hung like a curtain of fine links between me and my desire. I examined the walls; I found them to my surprise to be already covered with wallpaper, and I found the wallpaper to be already covered with uninteresting images, all bearing a ridiculous resemblance to each other. I could not understand why one arbitrary symbol (a symbol apparently entirely devoid of any religious or philosophical significance) should thus be sprinkled all over my nice walls like a sort of small-pox. The Bible must be referring to wallpapers, I think, when it says, "Use not vain repetitions, as the Gentiles do." I found the Turkey carpet a mass of unmeaning colours, rather like the Turkish Empire, or like the sweetmeat called Turkish Delight. I do not exactly know what Turkish Delight really is; but I suppose it is Macedonian Massacres. Everywhere that I went forlornly, with my pencil or my paint brush, I found that others had unaccountably been before me, spoiling the walls, the curtains, and the furniture with their childish and barbaric designs.

Nowhere did I find a really clear space for sketching until this occasion when I prolonged beyond the proper limit the process of lying on my back in bed. Then the light of that white heaven broke upon my vision, that breadth of mere white which is indeed almost the definition of Paradise, since it means purity and also means freedom. But alas! like all heavens, now that it is seen it is found to be unattainable; it looks more austere and more distant than the blue sky outside the window. For my proposal to paint on it with the bristly end of a broom has been discouraged—never mind by whom; by a person debarred from all political rights—and even my minor proposal to put the other end of the broom into the kitchen fire and turn it to charcoal has not been conceded. Yet I am certain that it was from persons in my position that all the original inspiration came for covering the ceilings of palaces and cathedrals with a riot of fallen angels or victorious gods. I am sure that it was only because Michael Angelo was engaged in the ancient and honourable occupation of lying in bed that he ever realized how the roof of the Sistine Chapel might be made into an awful imitation of a divine drama that could only be acted in the heavens.

The tone now commonly taken toward the practice of lying in bed is hypocritical and unhealthy. Of all the marks of modernity that seem to mean a kind of decadence, there is none more menacing and dangerous than the exultation of very small and secondary matters of conduct at the expense of very great and primary ones, at the expense of eternal ties and tragic human morality. If there is one thing worse than the modern weakening of major morals, it is the modern strengthening of minor morals. Thus it is considered more withering to accuse a man of bad taste than of bad ethics. Cleanliness is not next to godliness nowadays, for cleanliness is made essential and godliness is regarded as an offence. A playwright can attack the institution of marriage so long as he does not misrepresent the manners of society, and I have met Ibsenite pessimists who thought it wrong to take beer but right to take prussic acid. Especially this is so in matters of hygiene; notably such matters as lying in bed. Instead of being regarded, as it ought to be, as a matter of personal convenience and adjustment, it has come to be regarded by many as if it were a part of essential morals to get up early in the morning. It is upon the whole part of practical wisdom; but there is nothing good about it or bad about its opposite.

MISERS GET UP EARLY IN the morning; and burglars, I am informed, get up the night before. It is the great peril of our society that all its mechanisms may grow more fixed while its spirit grows more fickle. A man's minor actions and arrangements ought to be free, flexible, creative; the things that should be unchangeable are his principles, his ideals. But with us the reverse is true; our views change constantly; but our lunch does not change. Now, I should like men to have strong and rooted conceptions, but as for their lunch, let them have it sometimes in the garden, sometimes in bed, sometimes on the roof, sometimes in the top of a tree. Let them argue from the same first principles, but let them do it in a bed, or a boat, or a balloon. This alarming growth of good habits really means a too great emphasis on those virtues which mere custom can ensure, it means too little emphasis on those virtues which custom can never quite ensure, sudden and splendid virtues of inspired pity or of inspired candour. If ever that abrupt appeal is made to us we may fail. A man can get use to getting up at five o'clock in the morning. A man cannot very well get used to being burnt for his opinions; the first experiment is commonly fatal. Let us pay a little more attention to these possibilities of the heroic and unexpected. I dare say that when I get out of this bed I shall do some deed of an almost terrible virtue.

For those who study the great art of lying in bed there is one emphatic caution to be added. Even for those who can do their work in bed (like journalists), still more for those whose work cannot be done in bed (as, for example, the professional harpooners of whales), it is obvious that the indulgence must be very occasional. But that is not the caution I mean. The caution is this: if you do lie in bed, be sure you do it without any reason or justification at all. I do not speak, of course, of the seriously sick. But if a healthy man lies in bed, let him do it without a rag of excuse; then he will get up a healthy man. If he does it for some secondary hygienic reason, if he has some scientific explanation, he may get up a hypochondriac.

XI

The Twelve Men

The other day, while I was meditating on morality and Mr. H. Pitt, I was, so to speak, snatched up and put into a jury box to try people. The snatching took some weeks, but to me it seemed something sudden and arbitrary. I was put into this box because I lived in Battersea, and my name began with a C. Looking round me, I saw that there were also summoned and in attendance in the court whole crowds and processions of men, all of whom lived in Battersea, and all of whose names began with a C.

It seems that they always summon jurymen in this sweeping alphabetical way. At one official blow, so to speak, Battersea is denuded of all its C's, and left to get on as best it can with the rest of the alphabet. A Cumberpatch is missing from one street—a Chizzolpop from another—three Chucksterfields from Chucksterfield House; the children are crying out for an absent Cadgerboy; the woman at the street corner is weeping for her Coffintop, and will not be comforted. We settle down with a rollicking ease into our seats (for we are a bold, devil-may-care race, the C's of Battersea), and an oath is administered to us in a totally inaudible manner by an individual resembling an Army surgeon in his second childhood. We understand, however, that we are to well and truly try the case between our sovereign lord the King and the prisoner at the bar, neither of whom has put in an appearance as yet.

Just when I was wondering whether the King and the prisoner were, perhaps, coming to an amicable understanding in some adjoining public house, the prisoner's head appears above the barrier of the dock; he is accused of stealing bicycles, and he is the living image of a great friend of mine. We go into the matter of the stealing of the bicycles. We do well and truly try the case between the King and the prisoner in the affair of the bicycles. And we come to the conclusion, after a brief but reasonable discussion, that the King is not in any way implicated. Then we pass on to a woman who neglected her children, and who looks as if somebody or something had neglected her. And I am one of those who fancy that something had.

All the time that the eye took in these light appearances and the brain passed these light criticisms, there was in the heart a barbaric pity and fear which men have never been able to utter from the beginning, but which is the power behind half the poems of the world. The mood cannot even adequately be suggested, except faintly by this statement that tragedy is the highest expression of the infinite value of human life. Never had I stood so close to pain; and never so far away from pessimism. Ordinarily, I should not have spoken of these dark emotions at all, for speech about them is too difficult; but I mention them now for a specific and particular reason to the statement of which I will proceed at once. I speak these feelings because out of the furnace of them there came a curious realisation of a political or social truth. I saw with a queer and indescribable kind of clearness what a jury really is, and why we must never let it go.

The trend of our epoch up to this time has been consistently towards specialism and professionalism. We tend to have trained soldiers because they fight better, trained singers because they sing better, trained dancers because they dance better, specially instructed laughers because they laugh better, and so on and so on. The principle has been applied to law and politics by innumerable modern writers. Many Fabians have insisted that a greater part of our political work should be performed by experts. Many legalists have declared that the untrained jury should be altogether supplanted by the trained Judge.

Now, IF THIS WORLD OF ours were really what is called reasonable, I do not know that there would be any fault to find with this. But the true result of all experience and the true foundation of all religion is this. That the four or five things that it is most practically essential that a man should know, are all of them what people call paradoxes. That is to say, that though we all find them in life to be mere plain truths, yet we cannot easily state them in words without being guilty of seeming verbal contradictions. One of them, for instance, is the unimpeachable platitude that the man who finds most pleasure for himself is often the man who least hunts for it. Another is the paradox of courage; the fact that the way to avoid death is not to have too much aversion to it. Whoever is careless enough of his bones to climb some hopeful cliff above the tide may save his bones by that carelessness. Whoever will lose his life, the same shall save it; an entirely practical and prosaic statement.

Now, one of these four or five paradoxes which should be taught to every infant prattling at his mother's knee is the following: That the more a man looks at a thing, the less he can see it, and the more a man learns a thing the less he knows it. The Fabian argument of the expert, that the man who is trained should be the man who is trusted would be absolutely unanswerable if it were really true that a man who studied a thing and practiced it every day went on seeing more and more of its significance. But he does not. He goes on seeing less and less of its significance. In the same way, alas! we all go on every day, unless we are continually goading ourselves into gratitude and humility, seeing less and less of the significance of the sky or the stones.

Now it is a terrible business to mark a man out for the vengeance of men. But it is a thing to which a man can grow accustomed, as he can to other terrible things; he can even grow accustomed to the sun. And the horrible thing about all legal officials, even the best, about all judges, magistrates, barristers, detectives, and policemen, is not that they are wicked (some of them are good), not that they are stupid (several of them are quite intelligent), it is simply that they have got used to it.

Strictly they do not see the prisoner in the dock; all they see is the usual man in the usual place. They do not see the awful court of judgment; they only see their own workshop. Therefore, the instinct of Christian civilisation has most wisely declared that into their judgments there shall upon every occasion be infused fresh blood and fresh thoughts from the streets. Men shall come in who can see the court and the crowd, and coarse faces of the policeman and the professional criminals, the wasted faces of the wastrels, the unreal faces of the gesticulating counsel, and see it all as one sees a new picture or a play hitherto unvisited.

Our civilisation has decided, and very justly decided, that determining the guilt or innocence of men is a thing too important to be trusted to trained men. It wishes for light upon that awful matter, it asks men who know no more law than I know, but who can feel the things that I felt in the jury box. When it wants a library catalogued, or the solar system discovered, or any trifle of that kind, it uses up specialists. But when it wishes anything done which is really serious, it collects twelve of the ordinary men standing round. The same thing was done, if I remember right, by the Founder of Christianity.

XII

The Wind and the Trees

I am sitting under tall trees, with a great wind boiling like surf about the tops of them, so that their living load of leaves rocks and roars in something that is at once exultation and agony. I feel, in fact, as if I were actually sitting at the bottom of the sea among mere anchors and ropes, while over my head and over the green twilight of water sounded the everlasting rush of waves and the toil and crash and shipwreck of tremendous ships. The wind tugs at the trees as if it might pluck them root and all out of the earth like tufts of grass. Or, to try yet another desperate figure of speech for this unspeakable energy, the trees are straining and tearing and lashing as if they were a tribe of dragons each tied by the tail.

As I look at these top-heavy giants tortured by an invisible and violent witchcraft, a phrase comes back into my mind. I remember a little boy of my acquaintance who was once walking in Battersea Park under just such torn skies and tossing trees. He did not like the wind at all; it blew in his face too much; it made him shut his eyes; and it blew off his hat, of which he was very proud. He was, as far as I remember, about four. After complaining repeatedly of the atmospheric unrest, he said at last to his mother, "Well, why don't you take away the trees, and then it wouldn't wind."

Nothing could be more intelligent or natural than this mistake. Any one looking for the first time at the trees might fancy that they were indeed vast and titanic fans, which by their mere waving agitated the air around them for miles. Nothing, I say, could be more human and excusable than the belief that it is the trees which make the wind. Indeed, the belief is so human and excusable that it is, as a matter of fact, the belief of about ninety-nine out of a hundred of the philosophers, reformers, sociologists, and politicians of the great age in which we live. My small friend was, in fact, very like the principal modern thinkers; only much nicer.

IN THE LITTLE APOLOGUE OR parable which he has thus the honour of inventing, the trees stand for all visible things and the wind for the invisible. The wind is the spirit which bloweth where it listeth; the trees are the material things of the world which are blown where the spirit lists. The wind is philosophy, religion, revolution; the trees are cities and civilisations. We only know that there is a wind because the trees on some distant hill suddenly go mad. We only know that there is a real revolution because all the chimney-pots go mad on the whole skyline of the city.

Just as the ragged outline of a tree grows suddenly more ragged and rises into fantastic crests or tattered tails, so the human city rises under the wind of the spirit into toppling temples or sudden spires. No man has ever seen a revolution. Mobs pouring through the palaces, blood pouring down the gutters, the guillotine lifted higher than the throne, a prison in ruins, a people in arms—these things are not revolution, but the results of revolution.

You cannot see a wind; you can only see that there is a wind. So, also, you cannot see a revolution; you can only see that there is a revolution. And there never has been in the history of the world a real revolution, brutally active and decisive, which was not preceded by unrest and new dogma in the reign of invisible things. All revolutions began by being abstract. Most revolutions began by being quite pedantically abstract.

The wind is up above the world before a twig on the tree has moved. So there must always be a battle in the sky before there is a battle on the earth. Since it is lawful to pray for the coming of the kingdom, it is lawful also to pray for the coming of the revolution that shall restore the kingdom. It is lawful to hope to hear the wind of Heaven in the trees. It is lawful to pray "Thine anger come on earth as it is in Heaven."

THE GREAT HUMAN DOGMA, THEN, is that the wind moves the trees. The great human heresy is that the trees move the wind. When people begin to say that the material circumstances have alone created the moral circumstances, then they have prevented all possibility of serious change. For if my circumstances have made me wholly stupid, how can I be certain even that I am right in altering those circumstances?

The man who represents all thought as an accident of environment is simply smashing and discrediting all his own thoughts—including that one. To treat the human mind as having an ultimate authority is necessary to any kind of thinking, even free thinking. And nothing will ever be reformed in this age or country unless we realise that the moral fact comes first.

For example, most of us, I suppose, have seen in print and heard in debating clubs an endless discussion that goes on between Socialists and total abstainers. The latter say that drink leads to poverty; the former say that poverty leads to drink. I can only wonder at their either of them being content with such simple physical explanations. Surely it is obvious that the thing which among the English proletariat leads to poverty is the same as the thing which leads to drink; the absence of strong civic dignity, the absence of an instinct that resists degradation.

When you have discovered why enormous English estates were not long ago cut up into small holdings like the land of France, you will have discovered why the Englishman is more drunken than the Frenchman. The Englishman, among his million delightful virtues, really has this quality, which may strictly be called "hand to mouth," because under its influence a man's hand automatically seeks his own mouth, instead of seeking (as it sometimes should do) his oppressor's nose. And a man who says that the English inequality in land is due only to economic causes, or that the drunkenness of England is due only to economic causes, is saying something so absurd that he cannot really have thought what he was saying.

Yet things quite as preposterous as this are said and written under the influence of that great spectacle of babyish helplessness, the economic theory of history. We have people who represent that all great historic motives were economic, and then have to howl at the top of their voices in order to induce the modern democracy to act on economic motives. The extreme Marxian politicians in England exhibit themselves as a small, heroic minority, trying vainly to induce the world to do what, according to their theory, the world always does. The truth is, of course, that there will be a social revolution the moment the thing has ceased to be purely economic. You can never have a revolution in order to establish a democracy. You must have a democracy in order to have a revolution.

I GET UP FROM UNDER the trees, for the wind and the slight rain have ceased. The trees stand up like golden pillars in a clear sunlight. The tossing of the trees and the blowing of the wind have ceased simultaneously. So I suppose there are still modern philosophers who will maintain that the trees make the wind.

XIII

The Dickensian

He was a quiet man, dressed in dark clothes, with a large limp straw hat; with something almost military in his moustache and whiskers, but with a quite unmilitary stoop and very dreamy eyes. He was gazing with a rather gloomy interest at the cluster, one might almost say the tangle, of small shipping which grew thicker as our little pleasure boat crawled up into Yarmouth Harbour. A boat entering this harbour, as every one knows, does not enter in front of the town like a foreigner, but creeps round at the back like a traitor taking the town in the rear. The passage of the river seems almost too narrow for traffic, and in consequence the bigger ships look colossal. As we passed under a timber ship from Norway, which seemed to block up the heavens like a cathedral, the man in a straw hat pointed to an odd wooden figurehead carved like a woman, and said, like one continuing a conversation, "Now, why have they left off having them. They didn't do any one any harm?"

I replied with some flippancy about the captain's wife being jealous; but I knew in my heart that the man had struck a deep note. There has been something in our most recent civilisation which is mysteriously hostile to such healthy and humane symbols.

"They hate anything like that, which is human and pretty," he continued, exactly echoing my thoughts. "I believe they broke up all the jolly old figureheads with hatchets and enjoyed doing it."

"Like Mr. Quilp," I answered, "when he battered the wooden Admiral with the poker."

His whole face suddenly became alive, and for the first time he stood erect and stared at me.

"Do you come to Yarmouth for that?" he asked.

"For what?"

"For Dickens," he answered, and drummed with his foot on the deck.

"No," I answered; "I come for fun, though that is much the same thing."

"I always come," he answered quietly, "to find Peggotty's boat. It isn't here."

And when he said that I understood him perfectly.

There are two Yarmouths; I daresay there are two hundred to the people who live there. I myself have never come to the end of the list of Batterseas. But there are two to the stranger and tourist; the poor part, which is dignified, and the prosperous part, which is savagely vulgar. My new friend haunted the first of these like a ghost; to the latter he would only distantly allude.

"The place is very much spoilt now. . . trippers, you know," he would say, not at all scornfully, but simply sadly. That was the nearest he would go to an admission of the monstrous watering place that lay along the front, outblazing the sun, and more deafening than the sea. But behind—out of earshot of this uproar—there are lanes so narrow that they seem like secret entrances to some hidden place of repose. There are squares so brimful of silence that to plunge into one of them is like plunging into a pool. In these places the man and I paced up and down talking about Dickens, or, rather, doing what all true Dickensians do, telling each other verbatim long passages which both of us knew quite well already. We were really in the atmosphere of the older England. Fishermen passed us who might well have been characters like Peggotty; we went into a musty curiosity shop and bought pipe-stoppers carved into figures from Pickwick. The evening was settling down between all the buildings with that slow gold that seems to soak everything when we went into the church.

In the growing darkness of the church, my eye caught the coloured windows which on that clear golden evening were flaming with all the passionate heraldry of the most fierce and ecstatic of Christian arts. At length I said to my companion:

"Do you see that angel over there? I think it must be meant for the angel at the sepulchre."

He saw that I was somewhat singularly moved, and he raised his eyebrows.

"I daresay," he said. "What is there odd about that?"

After a pause I said, "Do you remember what the angel at the sepulchre said?"

"Not particularly," he answered; "but where are you off to in such a hurry?"

I walked him rapidly out of the still square, past the fishermen's almshouses, towards the coast, he still inquiring indignantly where I was going.

"I am going," I said, "to put pennies in automatic machines on the beach. I am going to listen to the niggers. I am going to have my photograph taken. I am going to drink ginger-beer out of its original bottle. I will buy some picture postcards. I do want a boat. I am ready to listen to a concertina, and but for the defects of my education should be ready to play it. I am willing to ride on a donkey; that is, if the donkey is willing. I am willing to be a donkey; for all this was commanded me by the angel in the stained-glass window."

"I really think," said the Dickensian, "that I had better put you in charge of your relations."

"Sir," I answered, "there are certain writers to whom humanity owes much, whose talent is yet of so shy or delicate or retrospective a type that we do well to link it with certain quaint places or certain perishing associations. It would not be unnatural to look for the spirit of Horace Walpole at Strawberry Hill, or even for the shade of Thackeray in Old Kensington. But let us have no antiquarianism about Dickens, for Dickens is not an antiquity. Dickens looks not backward, but forward; he might look at our modern mobs with satire, or with fury, but he would love to look at them. He might lash our democracy, but it would be because, like a democrat, he asked much from it. We will not have all his books bound up under the title of 'The Old Curiosity Shop.' Rather we will have them all bound up under the title of 'Great Expectations.' Wherever humanity is he would have us face it and make something of it, swallow it with a holy cannibalism, and assimilate it with the digestion of a giant. We must take these trippers as he would have taken them, and tear out of them their tragedy and their farce. Do you remember now what the angel said at the sepulchre? 'Why seek ye the living among the dead? He is not here; he is risen.'"

With that we came out suddenly on the wide stretch of the sands, which were black with the knobs and masses of our laughing and quite desperate democracy. And the sunset, which was now in its final glory, flung far over all of them a red flush and glitter like the gigantic firelight of Dickens. In that strange evening light every figure looked at once grotesque and attractive, as if he had a story to tell. I heard a little girl (who was being throttled by another little girl) say by way of self-vindication, "My sister-in-law 'as got four rings aside her weddin' ring!"

I stood and listened for more, but my friend went away.

XIV

In Topsy-Turvy Land

L ast week, in an idle metaphor, I took the tumbling of trees and the secret energy of the wind as typical of the visible world moving under the violence of the invisible. I took this metaphor merely because I happened to be writing the article in a wood. Nevertheless, now that I return to Fleet Street (which seems to me, I confess, much better and more poetical than all the wild woods in the world), I am strangely haunted by this accidental comparison. The people's figures seem a forest and their soul a wind. All the human personalities which speak or signal to me seem to have this fantastic character of the fringe of the forest against the sky. That man that talks to me, what is he but an articulate tree? That driver of a van who waves his hands wildly at me to tell me to get out of the way, what is he but a bunch of branches stirred and swayed by a spiritual wind, a sylvan object that I can continue to contemplate with calm? That policeman who lifts his hand to warn three omnibuses of the peril that they run in encountering my person, what is he but a shrub shaken for a moment with that blast of human law which is a thing stronger than anarchy? Gradually this impression of the woods wears off. But this black-and-white contrast between the visible and invisible, this deep sense that the one essential belief is belief in the invisible as against the visible, is suddenly and sensationally brought back to my mind. Exactly at the moment when Fleet Street has grown most familiar (that is, most bewildering and bright), my eye catches a poster of vivid violet, on which I see written in large black letters these remarkable words: "Should Shop Assistants Marry?"

When I saw those words everything might just as well have turned upside down. The men in Fleet Street might have been walking about on their hands. The cross of St. Paul's might have been hanging in the air upside down. For I realise that I have really come into a topsy-turvy country; I have come into the country where men do definitely believe that the waving of the trees makes the wind. That is to say, they believe that the material circumstances, however black and twisted, are more important than the spiritual realities, however powerful and pure. "Should Shop Assistants Marry?" I am puzzled to think what some periods and schools of human history would have made of such a question. The ascetics of the East or of some periods of the early Church would have thought that the question meant, "Are not shop assistants too saintly, too much of another world, even to feel the emotions of the sexes?" But I suppose that is not what the purple poster means. In some pagan cities it might have meant, "Shall slaves so vile as shop assistants even be allowed to propagate their abject race?" But I suppose that is not what the purple poster meant. We must face, I fear, the full insanity of what it does mean. It does really mean that a section of the human race is asking whether the primary relations of the two human sexes are particularly good for modern shops. The human race is asking whether Adam and Eve are entirely suitable for Marshall and Snelgrove. If this is not topsy-turvy I cannot imagine what would be. We ask whether the universal institution will improve our (please God) temporary institution. Yet I have known many such questions. For instance, I have known a man ask seriously, "Does Democracy help the Empire?" Which is like saying, "Is art favourable to frescoes?"

I say that there are many such questions asked. But if the world ever runs short of them, I can suggest a large number of questions of precisely the same kind, based on precisely the same principle.

"Do Feet Improve Boots?"—"Is Bread Better when Eaten?"— "Should Hats have Heads in them?"—"Do People Spoil a Town?"—"Do Walls Ruin Wall-papers?"—"Should Neckties enclose Necks?"—"Do Hands Hurt Walking-sticks?"—"Does Burning Destroy Firewood?"— "Is Cleanliness Good for Soap?"—"Can Cricket Really Improve Cricket-bats?"—"Shall We Take Brides with our Wedding Rings?" and a hundred others.

Not one of these questions differs at all in intellectual purport or in intellectual value from the question which I have quoted from the purple poster, or from any of the typical questions asked by half of the earnest economists of our times. All the questions they ask are of this character; they are all tinged with this same initial absurdity. They do not ask if the means is suited to the end; they all ask (with profound and penetrating scepticism) if the end is suited to the means. They do not ask whether the tail suits the dog. They all ask whether a dog is (by the highest artistic canons) the most ornamental appendage that can be put at the end of a tail. In short, instead of asking whether our modern arrangements, our streets, trades, bargains, laws, and

G.K. CHESTERTON

concrete institutions are suited to the primal and permanent idea of a healthy human life, they never admit that healthy human life into the discussion at all, except suddenly and accidentally at odd moments; and then they only ask whether that healthy human life is suited to our streets and trades. Perfection may be attainable or unattainable as an end. It may or may not be possible to talk of imperfection as a means to perfection. But surely it passes toleration to talk of perfection as a means to imperfection. The New Jerusalem may be a reality. It may be a dream. But surely it is too outrageous to say that the New Jerusalem is a reality on the road to Birmingham.

THIS IS THE MOST ENORMOUS and at the same time the most secret of the modern tyrannies of materialism. In theory the thing ought to be simple enough. A really human human being would always put the spiritual things first. A walking and speaking statue of God finds himself at one particular moment employed as a shop assistant. He has in himself a power of terrible love, a promise of paternity, a thirst for some loyalty that shall unify life, and in the ordinary course of things he asks himself, "How far do the existing conditions of those assisting in shops fit in with my evident and epic destiny in the matter of love and marriage?" But here, as I have said, comes in the quiet and crushing power of modern materialism. It prevents him rising in rebellion, as he would otherwise do. By perpetually talking about environment and visible things, by perpetually talking about economics and physical necessity, painting and keeping repainted a perpetual picture of iron machinery and merciless engines, of rails of steel, and of towers of stone, modern materialism at last produces this tremendous impression in which the truth is stated upside down. At last the result is achieved. The man does not say as he ought to have said, "Should married men endure being modern shop assistants?" The man says, "Should shop assistants marry?" Triumph has completed the immense illusion of materialism. The slave does not say, "Are these chains worthy of me?" The slave says scientifically and contentedly, "Am I even worthy of these chains?"

XV

What I Found in My Pocket

Once when I was very young I met one of those men who have made the Empire what it is—a man in an astracan coat, with an astracan moustache—a tight, black, curly moustache. Whether he put on the moustache with the coat or whether his Napoleonic will enabled him not only to grow a moustache in the usual place, but also to grow little moustaches all over his clothes, I do not know. I only remember that he said to me the following words: "A man can't get on nowadays by hanging about with his hands in his pockets." I made reply with the quite obvious flippancy that perhaps a man got on by having his hands in other people's pockets; whereupon he began to argue about Moral Evolution, so I suppose what I said had some truth in it. But the incident now comes back to me, and connects itself with another incident—if you can call it an incident—which happened to me only the other day.

I have only once in my life picked a pocket, and then (perhaps through some absent-mindedness) I picked my own. My act can really with some reason be so described. For in taking things out of my own pocket I had at least one of the more tense and quivering emotions of the thief; I had a complete ignorance and a profound curiosity as to what I should find there. Perhaps it would be the exaggeration of eulogy to call me a tidy person. But I can always pretty satisfactorily account for all my possessions. I can always tell where they are, and what I have done with them, so long as I can keep them out of my pockets. If once anything slips into those unknown abysses, I wave it a sad Virgilian farewell. I suppose that the things that I have dropped into my pockets are still there; the same presumption applies to the things that I have dropped into the sea. But I regard the riches stored in both these bottomless chasms with the same reverent ignorance. They tell us that on the last day the sea will give up its dead; and I suppose that on the same occasion long strings of extraordinary things will come running out of my pockets. But I have quite forgotten what any of them are; and there is really nothing (excepting the money) that I shall be at all surprised at finding among them.

SUCH AT LEAST HAS HITHERTO been my state of innocence. I here only wish briefly to recall the special, extraordinary, and hitherto unprecedented circumstances which led me in cold blood, and being of sound mind, to turn out my pockets. I was locked up in a third-class carriage for a rather long journey. The time was towards evening, but it might have been anything, for everything resembling earth or sky or light or shade was painted out as if with a great wet brush by an unshifting sheet of quite colourless rain. I had no books or newspapers. I had not even a pencil and a scrap of paper with which to write a religious epic. There were no advertisements on the walls of the carriage, otherwise I could have plunged into the study, for any collection of printed words is quite enough to suggest infinite complexities of mental ingenuity. When I find myself opposite the words "Sunlight Soap" I can exhaust all the aspects of Sun Worship, Apollo, and Summer poetry before I go on to the less congenial subject of soap. But there was no printed word or picture anywhere; there was nothing but blank wood inside the carriage and blank wet without. Now I deny most energetically that anything is, or can be, uninteresting. So I stared at the joints of the walls and seats, and began thinking hard on the fascinating subject of wood. Just as I had begun to realise why, perhaps, it was that Christ was a carpenter, rather than a bricklayer, or a baker, or anything else, I suddenly started upright, and remembered my pockets. I was carrying about with me an unknown treasury. I had a British Museum and a South Kensington collection of unknown curios hung all over me in different places. I began to take the things out.

THE FIRST THING I CAME upon consisted of piles and heaps of Battersea tram tickets. There were enough to equip a paper chase. They shook down in showers like confetti. Primarily, of course, they touched my patriotic emotions, and brought tears to my eyes; also they provided me with the printed matter I required, for I found on the back of them some short but striking little scientific essays about some kind of pill. Comparatively speaking, in my then destitution, those tickets might be regarded as a small but well-chosen scientific library. Should my railway journey continue (which seemed likely at the time) for a few months longer, I could imagine myself throwing myself into the controversial aspects of the pill, composing replies and rejoinders pro and con upon the data furnished to me. But after all it was the symbolic quality of the tickets that moved me most. For as certainly as the cross of St. George means English patriotism, those scraps of paper meant all that municipal patriotism which is now, perhaps, the greatest hope of England.

The next thing that I took out was a pocket-knife. A pocket-knife, I need hardly say, would require a thick book full of moral meditations all to itself. A knife typifies one of the most primary of those practical origins upon which as upon low, thick pillows all our human civilisation reposes. Metals, the mystery of the thing called iron and of the thing called steel, led me off half-dazed into a kind of dream. I saw into the intrails of dim, damp wood, where the first man among all the common stones found the strange stone. I saw a vague and violent battle, in which stone axes broke and stone knives were splintered against something shining and new in the hand of one desperate man. I heard all the hammers on all the anvils of the earth. I saw all the swords of Feudal and all the weals of Industrial war. For the knife is only a short sword; and the pocket-knife is a secret sword. I opened it and looked at that brilliant and terrible tongue which we call a blade; and I thought that perhaps it was the symbol of the oldest of the needs of man. The next moment I knew that I was wrong; for the thing that came next out of my pocket was a box of matches. Then I saw fire, which is stronger even than steel, the old, fierce female thing, the thing we all love, but dare not touch.

The next thing I found was a piece of chalk; and I saw in it all the art and all the frescoes of the world. The next was a coin of a very modest value; and I saw in it not only the image and superscription of our own Caesar, but all government and order since the world began. But I have not space to say what were the items in the long and splendid procession of poetical symbols that came pouring out. I cannot tell you all the things that were in my pocket. I can tell you one thing, however, that I could not find in my pocket. I allude to my railway ticket.

XVI

The Dragon's Grandmother

I met a man the other day who did not believe in fairy tales. I do not mean that he did not believe in the incidents narrated in them— that he did not believe that a pumpkin could turn into a coach. He did, indeed, entertain this curious disbelief. And, like all the other people I have ever met who entertained it, he was wholly unable to give me an intelligent reason for it. He tried the laws of nature, but he soon dropped that. Then he said that pumpkins were unalterable in ordinary experience, and that we all reckoned on their infinitely protracted pumpkinity. But I pointed out to him that this was not an attitude we adopt specially towards impossible marvels, but simply the attitude we adopt towards all unusual occurrences. If we were certain of miracles we should not count on them. Things that happen very seldom we all leave out of our calculations, whether they are miraculous or not. I do not expect a glass of water to be turned into wine; but neither do I expect a glass of water to be poisoned with prussic acid. I do not in ordinary business relations act on the assumption that the editor is a fairy; but neither do I act on the assumption that he is a Russian spy, or the lost heir of the Holy Roman Empire. What we assume in action is not that the natural order is unalterable, but simply that it is much safer to bet on uncommon incidents than on common ones. This does not touch the credibility of any attested tale about a Russian spy or a pumpkin turned into a coach. If I had seen a pumpkin turned into a Panhard motor-car with my own eyes that would not make me any more inclined to assume that the same thing would happen again. I should not invest largely in pumpkins with an eye to the motor trade. Cinderella got a ball dress from the fairy; but I do not suppose that she looked after her own clothes any the less after it.

But the view that fairy tales cannot really have happened, though crazy, is common. The man I speak of disbelieved in fairy tales in an even more amazing and perverted sense. He actually thought that fairy tales ought not to be told to children. That is (like a belief in slavery or annexation) one of those intellectual errors which lie very near to ordinary mortal sins. There are some refusals which, though they may be done what is called conscientiously, yet carry so much of their whole horror in the very act of them, that a man must in doing them not only harden but slightly corrupt his heart. One of them was the refusal of milk to young mothers when their husbands were in the field against us. Another is the refusal of fairy tales to children.

The man had come to see me in connection with some silly society of which I am an enthusiastic member; he was a fresh-coloured, short-sighted young man, like a stray curate who was too helpless even to find his way to the Church of England. He had a curious green necktie and a very long neck; I am always meeting idealists with very long necks. Perhaps it is that their eternal aspiration slowly lifts their heads nearer and nearer to the stars. Or perhaps it has something to do with the fact that so many of them are vegetarians: perhaps they are slowly evolving the neck of the giraffe so that they can eat all the tops of the trees in Kensington Gardens. These things are in every sense above me. Such, anyhow, was the young man who did not believe in fairy tales; and by a curious coincidence he entered the room when I had just finished looking through a pile of contemporary fiction, and had begun to read "Grimm's Fairy tales" as a natural consequence.

The modern novels stood before me, however, in a stack; and you can imagine their titles for yourself. There was "Suburban Sue: A Tale of Psychology," and also "Psychological Sue: A Tale of Suburbia"; there was "Trixy: A Temperament," and "Man-Hate: A Monochrome," and all those nice things. I read them with real interest, but, curiously enough, I grew tired of them at last, and when I saw "Grimm's Fairy Tales" lying accidentally on the table, I gave a cry of indecent joy. Here at least, here at last, one could find a little common sense. I opened the book, and my eyes fell on these splendid and satisfying words, "The Dragon's Grandmother." That at least was reasonable; that at least was true. "The Dragon's Grandmother!" While I was rolling this first touch of ordinary human reality upon my tongue, I looked up suddenly and saw this monster with a green tie standing in the doorway.

I listened to what he said about the society politely enough, I hope; but when he incidentally mentioned that he did not believe in fairy tales, I broke out beyond control. "Man," I said, "who are you that you should not believe in fairy tales? It is much easier to believe in Blue

Beard than to believe in you. A blue beard is a misfortune; but there are green ties which are sins. It is far easier to believe in a million fairy tales than to believe in one man who does not like fairy tales. I would rather kiss Grimm instead of a Bible and swear to all his stories as if they were thirty-nine articles than say seriously and out of my heart that there can be such a man as you; that you are not some temptation of the devil or some delusion from the void. Look at these plain, homely, practical words. 'The Dragon's Grandmother,' that is all right; that is rational almost to the verge of rationalism. If there was a dragon, he had a grandmother. But you—you had no grandmother! If you had known one, she would have taught you to love fairy tales. You had no father, you had no mother; no natural causes can explain you. You cannot be. I believe many things which I have not seen; but of such things as you it may be said, 'Blessed is he that has seen and yet has disbelieved.'"

IT SEEMED TO ME THAT he did not follow me with sufficient delicacy, so I moderated my tone. "Can you not see," I said, "that fairy tales in their essence are quite solid and straightforward; but that this everlasting fiction about modern life is in its nature essentially incredible? Folk-lore means that the soul is sane, but that the universe is wild and full of marvels. Realism means that the world is dull and full of routine, but that the soul is sick and screaming. The problem of the fairy tale is—what will a healthy man do with a fantastic world? The problem of the modern novel is—what will a madman do with a dull world? In the fairy tales the cosmos goes mad; but the hero does not go mad. In the modern novels the hero is mad before the book begins, and suffers from the harsh steadiness and cruel sanity of the cosmos. In the excellent tale of 'The Dragon's Grandmother,' in all the other tales of Grimm, it is assumed that the young man setting out on his travels will have all substantial truths in him; that he will be brave, full of faith, reasonable, that he will respect his parents, keep his word, rescue one kind of people, defy another kind, 'parcere subjectis et debellare,' etc. Then, having assumed this centre of sanity, the writer entertains himself by fancying what would happen if the whole world went mad all round it, if the sun turned green and the moon blue, if horses had six legs and giants had two heads. But your modern literature takes insanity as its centre. Therefore, it loses the interest even of insanity. A lunatic is not startling to himself, because he is quite serious; that is what makes him a lunatic. A man who thinks he is a piece of glass is to himself as dull as a piece of glass. A man who thinks he is a chicken is to himself as common as a chicken. It is only sanity that can see even a wild poetry in insanity. Therefore, these wise old tales made the hero ordinary and the tale extraordinary. But you have made the hero extraordinary and the tale ordinary—so ordinary—oh, so very ordinary."

I saw him still gazing at me fixedly. Some nerve snapped in me under the hypnotic stare. I leapt to my feet and cried, "In the name of God and Democracy and the Dragon's grandmother—in the name of all good things—I charge you to avaunt and haunt this house no more." Whether or no it was the result of the exorcism, there is no doubt that he definitely went away.

XVII

The Red Angel

I find that there really are human beings who think fairy tales bad for children. I do not speak of the man in the green tie, for him I can never count truly human. But a lady has written me an earnest letter saying that fairy tales ought not to be taught to children even if they are true. She says that it is cruel to tell children fairy tales, because it frightens them. You might just as well say that it is cruel to give girls sentimental novels because it makes them cry. All this kind of talk is based on that complete forgetting of what a child is like which has been the firm foundation of so many educational schemes. If you keep bogies and goblins away from children they would make them up for themselves. One small child in the dark can invent more hells than Swedenborg. One small child can imagine monsters too big and black to get into any picture, and give them names too unearthly and cacophonous to have occurred in the cries of any lunatic. The child, to begin with, commonly likes horrors, and he continues to indulge in them even when he does not like them. There is just as much difficulty in saying exactly where pure pain begins in his case, as there is in ours when we walk of our own free will into the torture-chamber of a great tragedy. The fear does not come from fairy tales; the fear comes from the universe of the soul.

THE TIMIDITY OF THE CHILD or the savage is entirely reasonable; they are alarmed at this world, because this world is a very alarming place. They dislike being alone because it is verily and indeed an awful idea to be alone. Barbarians fear the unknown for the same reason that Agnostics worship it—because it is a fact. Fairy tales, then, are not responsible for producing in children fear, or any of the shapes of fear; fairy tales do not give the child the idea of the evil or the ugly; that is in the child already, because it is in the world already. Fairy tales do not give the child his first idea of bogey. What fairy tales give the child is his first clear idea of the possible defeat of bogey. The baby has known the dragon intimately ever since he had an imagination. What the fairy tale provides for him is a St. George to kill the dragon.

Exactly what the fairy tale does is this: it accustoms him for a series of clear pictures to the idea that these limitless terrors had a limit, that these shapeless enemies have enemies in the knights of God, that there is something in the universe more mystical than darkness, and stronger than strong fear. When I was a child I have stared at the darkness until the whole black bulk of it turned into one negro giant taller than heaven. If there was one star in the sky it only made him a Cyclops. But fairy tales restored my mental health, for next day I read an authentic account of how a negro giant with one eye, of quite equal dimensions, had been baffled by a little boy like myself (of similar inexperience and even lower social status) by means of a sword, some bad riddles, and a brave heart. Sometimes the sea at night seemed as dreadful as any dragon. But then I was acquainted with many youngest sons and little sailors to whom a dragon or two was as simple as the sea.

Take the most horrible of Grimm's tales in incident and imagery, the excellent tale of the "Boy who Could not Shudder," and you will see what I mean. There are some living shocks in that tale. I remember specially a man's legs which fell down the chimney by themselves and walked about the room, until they were rejoined by the severed head and body which fell down the chimney after them. That is very good. But the point of the story and the point of the reader's feelings is not that these things are frightening, but the far more striking fact that the hero was not frightened at them. The most fearful of all these fearful wonders was his own absence of fear. He slapped the bogies on the back and asked the devils to drink wine with him; many a time in my youth, when stifled with some modern morbidity, I have prayed for a double portion of his spirit. If you have not read the end of his story, go and read it; it is the wisest thing in the world. The hero was at last taught to shudder by taking a wife, who threw a pail of cold water over him. In that one sentence there is more of the real meaning of marriage than in all the books about sex that cover Europe and America.

At the four corners of a child's bed stand Perseus and Roland, Sigurd and St. George. If you withdraw the guard of heroes you are not making him rational; you are only leaving him to fight the devils alone. For the devils, alas, we have always believed in. The hopeful element in the universe has in modern times continually been denied and reasserted; but the hopeless element has never for a moment been denied. As I told "H. N. B." (whom I pause to wish a Happy Christmas in its most superstitious sense), the one thing modern people really do believe in is damnation. The greatest of purely modern poets summed up the really modern attitude in that fine Agnostic line—

"There may be Heaven; there must be Hell."

The gloomy view of the universe has been a continuous tradition; and the new types of spiritual investigation or conjecture all begin by being gloomy. A little while ago men believed in no spirits. Now they are beginning rather slowly to believe in rather slow spirits.

SOME PEOPLE OBJECTED TO SPIRITUALISM, table rappings, and such things, because they were undignified, because the ghosts cracked jokes or waltzed with dinner-tables. I do not share this objection in the least. I wish the spirits were more farcical than they are. That they should make more jokes and better ones, would be my suggestion. For almost all the spiritualism of our time, in so far as it is new, is solemn and sad. Some Pagan gods were lawless, and some Christian saints were a little too serious; but the spirits of modern spiritualism are both lawless and serious—a disgusting combination. The specially contemporary spirits are not only devils, they are blue devils. This is, first and last, the real value of Christmas; in so far as the mythology remains at all it is a kind of happy mythology. Personally, of course, I believe in Santa Claus; but it is the season of forgiveness, and I will forgive others for not doing so. But if there is anyone who does not comprehend the defect in our world which I am civilising, I should recommend him, for instance, to read a story by Mr. Henry James, called "The Turn of the Screw." It is one of the most powerful things ever written, and it is one of the things about which I doubt most whether it ought ever to have been written at all. It describes two innocent children gradually growing at once omniscient and half-witted under the influence of the foul ghosts of a groom and a governess. As I say, I doubt whether Mr. Henry James ought to have published it (no, it is not indecent, do not buy it; it is a spiritual matter), but I think the question so doubtful that I will give that truly great man a chance. I will approve the thing as well as admire it if he will write another tale just as powerful about two children and Santa Claus. If he will not, or cannot, then the conclusion is clear; we can deal strongly with gloomy mystery, but not with happy mystery; we are not rationalists, but diabolists.

I HAVE THOUGHT VAGUELY OF all this staring at a great red fire that stands up in the room like a great red angel. But, perhaps, you have never heard of a red angel. But you have heard of a blue devil. That is exactly what I mean.

XVIII

THE TOWER

I have been standing where everybody has stood, opposite the great Belfry Tower of Bruges, and thinking, as every one has thought (though not, perhaps, said), that it is built in defiance of all decencies of architecture. It is made in deliberate disproportion to achieve the one startling effect of height. It is a church on stilts. But this sort of sublime deformity is characteristic of the whole fancy and energy of these Flemish cities. Flanders has the flattest and most prosaic landscapes, but the most violent and extravagant of buildings. Here Nature is tame; it is civilisation that is untamable. Here the fields are as flat as a paved square; but, on the other hand, the streets and roofs are as uproarious as a forest in a great wind. The waters of wood and meadow slide as smoothly and meekly as if they were in the London water-pipes. But the parish pump is carved with all the creatures out of the wilderness. Part of this is true, of course, of all art. We talk of wild animals, but the wildest animal is man. There are sounds in music that are more ancient and awful than the cry of the strangest beast at night. And so also there are buildings that are shapeless in their strength, seeming to lift themselves slowly like monsters from the primal mire, and there are spires that seem to fly up suddenly like a startled bird.

THIS SAVAGERY EVEN IN STONE is the expression of the special spirit in humanity. All the beasts of the field are respectable; it is only man who has broken loose. All animals are domestic animals; only man is ever undomestic. All animals are tame animals; it is only we who are wild. And doubtless, also, while this queer energy is common to all human art, it is also generally characteristic of Christian art among the arts of the world. This is what people really mean when they say that Christianity is barbaric, and arose in ignorance. As a matter of historic fact, it didn't; it arose in the most equably civilised period the world has ever seen.

But it is true that there is something in it that breaks the outline of perfect and conventional beauty, something that dots with anger the blind eyes of the Apollo and lashes to a cavalry charge the horses of the

Elgin Marbles. Christianity is savage, in the sense that it is primeval; there is in it a touch of the nigger hymn. I remember a debate in which I had praised militant music in ritual, and some one asked me if I could imagine Christ walking down the street before a brass band. I said I could imagine it with the greatest ease; for Christ definitely approved a natural noisiness at a great moment. When the street children shouted too loud, certain priggish disciples did begin to rebuke them in the name of good taste. He said: "If these were silent the very stones would cry out." With these words He called up all the wealth of artistic creation that has been founded on this creed. With those words He founded Gothic architecture. For in a town like this, which seems to have grown Gothic as a wood grows leaves, anywhere and anyhow, any odd brick or moulding may be carved off into a shouting face. The front of vast buildings is thronged with open mouths, angels praising God, or devils defying Him. Rock itself is racked and twisted, until it seems to scream. The miracle is accomplished; the very stones cry out.

But though this furious fancy is certainly a specialty of men among creatures, and of Christian art among arts, it is still most notable in the art of Flanders. All Gothic buildings are full of extravagant things in detail; but this is an extravagant thing in design. All Christian temples worth talking about have gargoyles; but Bruges Belfry is a gargoyle. It is an unnaturally long-necked animal, like a giraffe. The same impression of exaggeration is forced on the mind at every corner of a Flemish town. And if any one asks, "Why did the people of these flat countries instinctively raise these riotous and towering monuments?" the only answer one can give is, "Because they were the people of these flat countries." If any one asks, "Why the men of Bruges sacrificed architecture and everything to the sense of dizzy and divine heights?" we can only answer, "Because Nature gave them no encouragement to do so."

As I stare at the Belfry, I think with a sort of smile of some of my friends in London who are quite sure of how children will turn out if you give them what they call "the right environment." It is a troublesome thing, environment, for it sometimes works positively and sometimes negatively, and more often between the two. A beautiful environment may make a child love beauty; it may make him bored with beauty; most likely the two effects will mix and neutralise each other. Most likely, that is, the environment will make hardly any difference at all.

In the scientific style of history (which was recently fashionable, and is still conventional) we always had a list of countries that had owed their characteristics to their physical conditions.

The Spaniards (it was said) are passionate because their country is hot; Scandinavians adventurous because their country is cold; Englishmen naval because they are islanders; Switzers free because they are mountaineers. It is all very nice in its way. Only unfortunately I am quite certain that I could make up quite as long a list exactly contrary in its argument point-blank against the influence of their geographical environment. Thus Spaniards have discovered more continents than Scandinavians because their hot climate discouraged them from exertion. Thus Dutchmen have fought for their freedom quite as bravely as Switzers because the Dutch have no mountains. Thus Pagan Greece and Rome and many Mediterranean peoples have specially hated the sea because they had the nicest sea to deal with, the easiest sea to manage. I could extend the list for ever. But however long it was, two examples would certainly stand up in it as pre-eminent and unquestionable. The first is that the Swiss, who live under staggering precipices and spires of eternal snow, have produced no art or literature at all, and are by far the most mundane, sensible, and business-like people in Europe. The other is that the people of Belgium, who live in a country like a carpet, have, by an inner energy, desired to exalt their towers till they struck the stars.

As it is therefore quite doubtful whether a person will go specially with his environment or specially against his environment, I cannot comfort myself with the thought that the modern discussions about environment are of much practical value. But I think I will not write any more about these modern theories, but go on looking at the Belfry of Bruges. I would give them the greater attention if I were not pretty well convinced that the theories will have disappeared a long time before the Belfry.

XIX

How I Met the President

Several years ago, when there was a small war going on in South Africa and a great fuss going on in England, when it was by no means so popular and convenient to be a Pro-Boer as it is now, I remember making a bright suggestion to my Pro-Boer friends and allies, which was not, I regret to say, received with the seriousness it deserved. I suggested that a band of devoted and noble youths, including ourselves, should express our sense of the pathos of the President's and the Republic's fate by growing Kruger beards under our chins. I imagined how abruptly this decoration would alter the appearance of Mr. John Morley; how startling it would be as it emerged from under the chin of Mr. Lloyd-George. But the younger men, my own friends, on whom I more particularly urged it, men whose names are in many cases familiar to the readers of this paper—Mr. Masterman's for instance, and Mr. Conrad Noel—they, I felt, being young and beautiful, would do even more justice to the Kruger beard, and when walking down the street with it could not fail to attract attention. The beard would have been a kind of counterblast to the Rhodes hat. An appropriate counterblast; for the Rhodesian power in Africa is only an external thing, placed upon the top like a hat; the Dutch power and tradition is a thing rooted and growing like a beard; we have shaved it, and it is growing again. The Kruger beard would represent time and the natural processes. You cannot grow a beard in a moment of passion.

After making this proposal to my friends I hurriedly left town. I went down to a West Country place where there was shortly afterwards an election, at which I enjoyed myself very much canvassing for the Liberal candidate. The extraordinary thing was that he got in. I sometimes lie awake at night and meditate upon that mystery; but it must not detain us now. The rather singular incident which happened to me then, and which some recent events have recalled to me, happened while the canvassing was still going on. It was a burning blue day, and the warm sunshine, settling everywhere on the high hedges and the low hills, brought out into a kind of heavy bloom that Humane quality of the landscape which, as far as I know, only exists in England; that sense as if the bushes and the roads were human, and had kindness like men; as if the tree were a good giant with one wooden leg; as if the very line of palings were a row of good-tempered gnomes. On one side of the white, sprawling road a low hill or down showed but a little higher than the hedge, on the other the land tumbled down into a valley that opened towards the Mendip hills. The road was very erratic, for every true English road exists in order to lead one a dance; and what could be more beautiful and beneficent than a dance? At an abrupt turn of it I came upon a low white building, with dark doors and dark shuttered windows, evidently not inhabited and scarcely in the ordinary sense inhabitable—a thing more like a toolhouse than a house of any other kind. Made idle by the heat, I paused, and, taking a piece of red chalk out of my pocket, began drawing aimlessly on the back door—drawing goblins and Mr. Chamberlain, and finally the ideal Nationalist with the Kruger beard. The materials did not permit of any delicate rendering of his noble and national expansion of countenance (stoical and yet hopeful, full of tears for man, and yet of an element of humour); but the hat was finely handled. Just as I was adding the finishing touches to the Kruger fantasy, I was frozen to the spot with terror. The black door, which I thought no more of than the lid of an empty box, began slowly to open, impelled from within by a human hand. And President Kruger himself came out into the sunlight!

He was a shade milder of eye than he was in his portraits, and he did not wear that ceremonial scarf which was usually, in such pictures, slung across his ponderous form. But there was the hat which filled the Empire with so much alarm; there were the clumsy dark clothes, there was the heavy, powerful face; there, above all, was the Kruger beard which I had sought to evoke (if I may use the verb) from under the features of Mr. Masterman. Whether he had the umbrella or not I was too much emotionally shaken to observe; he had not the stone lions with him, or Mrs. Kruger; and what he was doing in that dark shed I cannot imagine, but I suppose he was oppressing an Outlander.

I was surprised, I must confess, to meet President Kruger in Somersetshire during the war. I had no idea that he was in the neighbourhood. But a yet more arresting surprise awaited me. Mr. Kruger regarded me for some moments with a dubious grey eye, and then addressed me with a strong Somersetshire accent. A curious cold shock went through me to hear that inappropriate voice coming out of that familiar form. It was as if you met a Chinaman, with pigtail and yellow jacket, and he began to talk broad Scotch. But the next moment, of course, I understood the situation. We had much underrated the Boers in supposing that the Boer education was incomplete. In pursuit of his ruthless plot against our island home, the terrible President had learnt not only English, but all the dialects at a moment's notice to win over a Lancashire merchant or seduce a Northumberland Fusilier. No doubt, if I asked him, this stout old gentleman could grind out Sussex, Essex, Norfolk, Suffolk, and so on, like the tunes in a barrel organ. I could not wonder if our plain, true-hearted German millionaires fell before a cunning so penetrated with culture as this.

AND NOW I COME TO the third and greatest surprise of all that this strange old man gave me. When he asked me, dryly enough, but not without a certain steady civility that belongs to old-fashioned country people, what I wanted and what I was doing, I told him the facts of the case, explaining my political mission and the almost angelic qualities of the Liberal candidate. Whereupon, this old man became suddenly transfigured in the sunlight into a devil of wrath. It was some time before I could understand a word he said, but the one word that kept on recurring was the word "Kruger," and it was invariably accompanied with a volley of violent terms. Was I for old Kruger, was I? Did I come to him and want him to help old Kruger? I ought to be ashamed, I was. . . and here he became once more obscure. The one thing that he made quite clear was that he wouldn't do anything for Kruger.

"But you ARE Kruger," burst from my lips, in a natural explosion of reasonableness. "You ARE Kruger, aren't you?"

After this innocent CRI DE COEUR of mine, I thought at first there would be a fight, and I remembered with regret that the President in early life had had a hobby of killing lions. But really I began to think that I had been mistaken, and that it was not the President after all. There was a confounding sincerity in the anger with which he declared that he was Farmer Bowles, and everybody knowed it. I appeased him eventually and parted from him at the door of his farmhouse, where he left me with a few tags of religion, which again raised my suspicions of his identity. In the coffee-room to which I returned there was an illustrated paper with a picture of President Kruger, and he and Farmer Bowles were as like as two peas. There was a picture also of a group of Outlander leaders, and the faces of them, leering and triumphant, were perhaps unduly darkened by the photograph, but they seemed to me like the faces of a distant and hostile people.

I saw the old man once again on the fierce night of the poll, when he drove down our Liberal lines in a little cart ablaze with the blue Tory ribbons, for he was a man who would carry his colours everywhere. It was evening, and the warm western light was on the grey hair and heavy massive features of that good old man. I knew as one knows a fact of sense that if Spanish and German stockbrokers had flooded his farm or country he would have fought them for ever, not fiercely like an Irishman, but with the ponderous courage and ponderous cunning of the Boer. I knew that without seeing it, as certainly as I knew without seeing it that when he went into the polling room he put his cross against the Conservative name. Then he came out again, having given his vote and looking more like Kruger than ever. And at the same hour on the same night thousands upon thousands of English Krugers gave the same vote. And thus Kruger was pulled down and the dark-faced men in the photograph reigned in his stead.

XX

The Giant

I sometimes fancy that every great city must have been built by night. At least, it is only at night that every part of a great city is great. All architecture is great architecture after sunset; perhaps architecture is really a nocturnal art, like the art of fireworks. At least, I think many people of those nobler trades that work by night (journalists, policemen, burglars, coffee-stall keepers, and such mistaken enthusiasts as refuse to go home till morning) must often have stood admiring some black bulk of building with a crown of battlements or a crest of spires and then burst into tears at daybreak to discover that it was only a haberdasher's shop with huge gold letters across the face of it.

I HAD A SENSATION OF this sort the other day as I happened to be wandering in the Temple Gardens towards the end of twilight. I sat down on a bench with my back to the river, happening to choose such a place that a huge angle and façade of building jutting out from the Strand sat above me like an incubus. I dare say that if I took the same seat to-morrow by daylight I should find the impression entirely false. In sunlight the thing might seem almost distant; but in that half-darkness it seemed as if the walls were almost falling upon me. Never before have I had so strongly the sense which makes people pessimists in politics, the sense of the hopeless height of the high places of the earth. That pile of wealth and power, whatever was its name, went up above and beyond me like a cliff that no living thing could climb. I had an irrational sense that this thing had to be fought, that I had to fight it; and that I could offer nothing to the occasion but an indolent journalist with a walking-stick.

Almost as I had the thought, two windows were lit in that black, blind face. It was as if two eyes had opened in the huge face of a sleeping giant; the eyes were too close together, and gave it the suggestion of a bestial sneer. And either by accident of this light or of some other, I could now read the big letters which spaced themselves across the front; it was the Babylon Hotel. It was the perfect symbol of everything that I should like to pull down with my hands if I could. Reared by a detected robber, it is framed to be the fashionable and luxurious home of undetected robbers. In the house of man are many mansions; but there is a class of men who feel normal nowhere except in the Babylon Hotel or in Dartmoor Gaol. That big black face, which was staring at me with its flaming eyes too close together, that was indeed the giant of all epic and fairy tales. But, alas! I was not the giant-killer; the hour had come, but not the man. I sat down on the seat again (I had had one wild impulse to climb up the front of the hotel and fall in at one of the windows), and I tried to think, as all decent people are thinking, what one can really do. And all the time that oppressive wall went up in front of me, and took hold upon the heavens like a house of the gods.

It is remarkable that in so many great wars it has been the defeated who have won. The people who were left worst at the end of the war were generally the people who were left best at the end of the whole business. For instance, the Crusades ended in the defeat of the Christians. But they did not end in the decline of the Christians; they ended in the decline of the Saracens. That huge prophetic wave of Moslem power which had hung in the very heavens above the towns of Christendom, that wave was broken, and never came on again. The Crusaders had saved Paris in the act of losing Jerusalem. The same applies to that epic of Republican war in the eighteenth century to which we Liberals owe our political creed. The French Revolution ended in defeat: the kings came back across a carpet of dead at Waterloo. The Revolution had lost its last battle; but it had gained its first object. It had cut a chasm. The world has never been the same since. No one after that has ever been able to treat the poor merely as a pavement.

These jewels of God, the poor, are still treated as mere stones of the street; but as stones that may sometimes fly. If it please God, you and I may see some of the stones flying again before we see death. But here I only remark the interesting fact that the conquered almost always conquer. Sparta killed Athens with a final blow, and she was born again. Sparta went away victorious, and died slowly of her own wounds. The Boers lost the South African War and gained South Africa.

And this is really all that we can do when we fight something really stronger than ourselves; we can deal it its death-wound one moment; it deals us death in the end. It is something if we can shock and jar the unthinking impetus and enormous innocence of evil; just as a pebble on a railway can stagger the Scotch express. It is enough for the great martyrs and criminals of the French revolution, that they have surprised for all time the secret weakness of the strong. They have awakened and set leaping and quivering in his crypt for ever the coward in the hearts of kings.

When Jack the Giant-Killer really first saw the giant his experience was not such as has been generally supposed. If you care to hear it I will tell you the real story of Jack the Giant-Killer. To begin with, the most awful thing which Jack first felt about the giant was that he was not a giant. He came striding across an interminable wooded plain, and against its remote horizon the giant was quite a small figure, like a figure in a picture—he seemed merely a man walking across the grass. Then Jack was shocked by remembering that the grass which the man was treading down was one of the tallest forests upon that plain. The man came nearer and nearer, growing bigger and bigger, and at the instant when he passed the possible stature of humanity Jack almost screamed. The rest was an intolerable apocalypse.

The giant had the one frightful quality of a miracle; the more he became incredible the more he became solid. The less one could believe in him the more plainly one could see him. It was unbearable that so much of the sky should be occupied by one human face. His eyes, which had stood out like bow windows, became bigger yet, and there was no metaphor that could contain their bigness; yet still they were human eyes. Jack's intellect was utterly gone under that huge hypnotism of the face that filled the sky; his last hope was submerged, his five wits all still with terror.

But there stood up in him still a kind of cold chivalry, a dignity of dead honour that would not forget the small and futile sword in his hand. He rushed at one of the colossal feet of this human tower, and when he came quite close to it the ankle-bone arched over him like a cave. Then he planted the point of his sword against the foot and leant on it with all his weight, till it went up to the hilt and broke the hilt, and then snapped just under it. And it was plain that the giant felt a sort of prick, for he snatched up his great foot into his great hand for an instant; and then, putting it down again, he bent over and stared at the ground until he had seen his enemy.

Then he picked up Jack between a big finger and thumb and threw him away; and as Jack went through the air he felt as if he were flying from system to system through the universe of stars. But, as the giant had thrown him away carelessly, he did not strike a stone, but struck soft mire by the side of a distant river. There he lay insensible for several hours; but when he awoke again his horrible conqueror was still in sight. He was striding away across the void and wooded plain towards where it ended in the sea; and by this time he was only much higher than any of the hills. He grew less and less indeed; but only as a really high mountain grows at last less and less when we leave it in a railway train. Half an hour afterwards he was a bright blue colour, as are the distant hills; but his outline was still human and still gigantic. Then the big blue figure seemed to come to the brink of the big blue sea, and even as it did so it altered its attitude. Jack, stunned and bleeding, lifted himself laboriously upon one elbow to stare. The giant once more caught hold of his ankle, wavered twice as in a wind, and then went over into the great sea which washes the whole world, and which, alone of all things God has made, was big enough to drown him.

XXI

A Great Man

People accuse journalism of being too personal; but to me it has always seemed far too impersonal. It is charged with tearing away the veils from private life; but it seems to me to be always dropping diaphanous but blinding veils between men and men. The Yellow Press is abused for exposing facts which are private; I wish the Yellow Press did anything so valuable. It is exactly the decisive individual touches that it never gives; and a proof of this is that after one has met a man a million times in the newspapers it is always a complete shock and reversal to meet him in real life. The Yellow Pressman seems to have no power of catching the first fresh fact about a man that dominates all after impressions. For instance, before I met Bernard Shaw I heard that he spoke with a reckless desire for paradox or a sneering hatred of sentiment; but I never knew till he opened his mouth that he spoke with an Irish accent, which is more important than all the other criticisms put together.

Journalism is not personal enough. So far from digging out private personalities, it cannot even report the obvious personalities on the surface. Now there is one vivid and even bodily impression of this kind which we have all felt when we met great poets or politicians, but which never finds its way into the newspapers. I mean the impression that they are much older than we thought they were. We connect great men with their great triumphs, which generally happened some years ago, and many recruits enthusiastic for the thin Napoleon of Marengo must have found themselves in the presence of the fat Napoleon of Leipzic.

I remember reading a newspaper account of how a certain rising politician confronted the House of Lords with the enthusiasm almost of boyhood. It described how his "brave young voice" rang in the rafters. I also remember that I met him some days after, and he was considerably older than my own father. I mention this truth for only one purpose: all this generalisation leads up to only one fact—the fact that I once met a great man who was younger than I expected.

I HAD COME OVER THE wooded wall from the villages about Epsom, and down a stumbling path between trees towards the valley in which

Dorking lies. A warm sunlight was working its way through the leafage; a sunlight which though of saintless gold had taken on the quality of evening. It was such sunlight as reminds a man that the sun begins to set an instant after noon. It seemed to lessen as the wood strengthened and the road sank.

I had a sensation peculiar to such entangled descents; I felt that the treetops that closed above me were the fixed and real things, certain as the level of the sea; but that the solid earth was every instant failing under my feet. In a little while that splendid sunlight showed only in splashes, like flaming stars and suns in the dome of green sky. Around me in that emerald twilight were trunks of trees of every plain or twisted type; it was like a chapel supported on columns of every earthly and unearthly style of architecture.

Without intention my mind grew full of fancies on the nature of the forest; on the whole philosophy of mystery and force. For the meaning of woods is the combination of energy with complexity. A forest is not in the least rude or barbarous; it is only dense with delicacy. Unique shapes that an artist would copy or a philosopher watch for years if he found them in an open plain are here mingled and confounded; but it is not a darkness of deformity. It is a darkness of life; a darkness of perfection. And I began to think how much of the highest human obscurity is like this, and how much men have misunderstood it. People will tell you, for instance, that theology became elaborate because it was dead. Believe me, if it had been dead it would never have become elaborate; it is only the live tree that grows too many branches.

THESE TREES THINNED AND FELL away from each other, and I came out into deep grass and a road. I remember being surprised that the evening was so far advanced; I had a fancy that this valley had a sunset all to itself. I went along that road according to directions that had been given me, and passed the gateway in a slight paling beyond which the wood changed only faintly to a garden. It was as if the curious courtesy and fineness of that character I was to meet went out from him upon the valley; for I felt on all these things the finger of that quality which the old English called "faërie"; it is the quality which those can never understand who think of the past as merely brutal; it is an ancient elegance such as there is in trees. I went through the garden and saw an old man sitting by a table, looking smallish in his big chair. He was already an invalid, and his hair and beard were both white; not like snow, for snow is cold and heavy, but like something feathery, or even fierce; rather they were white like the white thistledown. I came up quite close to him; he looked at me as he put out his frail hand, and I saw of a sudden that his eyes were startlingly young. He was the one great man of the old world whom I have met who was not a mere statue over his own grave.

He was deaf and he talked like a torrent. He did not talk about the books he had written; he was far too much alive for that. He talked about the books he had not written. He unrolled a purple bundle of romances which he had never had time to sell. He asked me to write one of the stories for him, as he would have asked the milkman, if he had been talking to the milkman. It was a splendid and frantic story, a sort of astronomical farce. It was all about a man who was rushing up to the Royal Society with the only possible way of avoiding an earth-destroying comet; and it showed how, even on this huge errand, the man was tripped up at every other minute by his own weakness and vanities; how he lost a train by trifling or was put in gaol for brawling. That is only one of them; there were ten or twenty more. Another, I dimly remember, was a version of the fall of Parnell; the idea that a quite honest man might be secret from a pure love of secrecy, of solitary self-control. I went out of that garden with a blurred sensation of the million possibilities of creative literature. The feeling increased as my way fell back into the wood; for a wood is a palace with a million corridors that cross each other everywhere. I really had the feeling that I had seen the creative quality; which is supernatural. I had seen what Virgil calls the Old Man of the Forest: I had seen an elf. The trees thronged behind my path; I have never seen him again; and now I shall not see him, because he died last Tuesday.

XXII

The Orthodox Barber

Those thinkers who cannot believe in any gods often assert that the love of humanity would be in itself sufficient for them; and so, perhaps, it would, if they had it. There is a very real thing which may be called the love of humanity; in our time it exists almost entirely among what are called uneducated people; and it does not exist at all among the people who talk about it.

A positive pleasure in being in the presence of any other human being is chiefly remarkable, for instance, in the masses on Bank Holiday; that is why they are so much nearer Heaven (despite appearances) than any other part of our population.

I remember seeing a crowd of factory girls getting into an empty train at a wayside country station. There were about twenty of them; they all got into one carriage; and they left all the rest of the train entirely empty. That is the real love of humanity. That is the definite pleasure in the immediate proximity of one's own kind. Only this coarse, rank, real love of men seems to be entirely lacking in those who propose the love of humanity as a substitute for all other love; honourable, rationalistic idealists.

I can well remember the explosion of human joy which marked the sudden starting of that train; all the factory girls who could not find seats (and they must have been the majority) relieving their feelings by jumping up and down. Now I have never seen any rationalistic idealists do this. I have never seen twenty modern philosophers crowd into one third-class carriage for the mere pleasure of being together. I have never seen twenty Mr. McCabes all in one carriage and all jumping up and down.

Some people express a fear that vulgar trippers will overrun all beautiful places, such as Hampstead or Burnham Beeches. But their fear is unreasonable; because trippers always prefer to trip together; they pack as close as they can; they have a suffocating passion of philanthropy.

BUT AMONG THE MINOR AND milder aspects of the same principle, I have no hesitation in placing the problem of the colloquial barber. Before any modern man talks with authority about loving men, I insist (I insist with violence) that he shall always be very much pleased when his barber tries to talk to him. His barber is humanity: let him love that. If he is not pleased at this, I will not accept any substitute in the way of interest in the Congo or the future of Japan. If a man cannot love his barber whom he has seen, how shall he love the Japanese whom he has not seen?

It is urged against the barber that he begins by talking about the weather; so do all dukes and diplomatists, only that they talk about it with ostentatious fatigue and indifference, whereas the barber talks about it with an astonishing, nay incredible, freshness of interest. It is objected to him that he tells people that they are going bald. That is to say, his very virtues are cast up against him; he is blamed because, being a specialist, he is a sincere specialist, and because, being a tradesman, he is not entirely a slave. But the only proof of such things is by example; therefore I will prove the excellence of the conversation of barbers by a specific case. Lest any one should accuse me of attempting to prove it by fictitious means, I beg to say quite seriously that though I forget the exact language employed, the following conversation between me and a human (I trust), living barber really took place a few days ago.

I HAD BEEN INVITED TO some At Home to meet the Colonial Premiers, and lest I should be mistaken for some partly reformed bush-ranger out of the interior of Australia I went into a shop in the Strand to get shaved. While I was undergoing the torture the man said to me:

"There seems to be a lot in the papers about this new shaving, sir. It seems you can shave yourself with anything—with a stick or a stone or a pole or a poker" (here I began for the first time to detect a sarcastic intonation) "or a shovel or a——"

Here he hesitated for a word, and I, although I knew nothing about the matter, helped him out with suggestions in the same rhetorical vein.

"Or a button-hook," I said, "or a blunderbuss or a battering-ram or a piston-rod—"

He resumed, refreshed with this assistance, "Or a curtain rod or a candle-stick, or a——"

"Cow-catcher," I suggested eagerly, and we continued in this ecstatic duet for some time. Then I asked him what it was all about, and he told me. He explained the thing eloquently and at length.

"The funny part of it is," he said, "that the thing isn't new at all. It's been talked about ever since I was a boy, and long before. There is always a notion that the razor might be done without somehow. But none of those schemes ever came to anything; and I don't believe myself that this will."

"Why, as to that," I said, rising slowly from the chair and trying to put on my coat inside out, "I don't know how it may be in the case of you and your new shaving. Shaving, with all respect to you, is a trivial and materialistic thing, and in such things startling inventions are sometimes made. But what you say reminds me in some dark and dreamy fashion of something else. I recall it especially when you tell me, with such evident experience and sincerity, that the new shaving is not really new. My friend, the human race is always trying this dodge of making everything entirely easy; but the difficulty which it shifts off one thing it shifts on to another. If one man has not the toil of preparing a man's chin, I suppose that some other man has the toil of preparing something very curious to put on a man's chin. It would be nice if we could be shaved without troubling anybody. It would be nicer still if we could go unshaved without annoying anybody—

> "'But, O wise friend, chief Barber of the Strand,
> Brother, nor you nor I have made the world.'

"Whoever made it, who is wiser, and we hope better than we, made it under strange limitations, and with painful conditions of pleasure.

"In the first and darkest of its books it is fiercely written that a man shall not eat his cake and have it; and though all men talked until the stars were old it would still be true that a man who has lost his razor could not shave with it. But every now and then men jump up with the new something or other and say that everything can be had without sacrifice, that bad is good if you are only enlightened, and that there is no real difference between being shaved and not being shaved. The difference, they say, is only a difference of degree; everything is evolutionary and relative. Shavedness is immanent in man. Every tenpenny nail is a Potential Razor. The superstitious people of the past (they say) believed that a lot of black bristles standing out at right angles to one's face was a positive affair. But the higher criticism teaches us better. Bristles are merely negative. They are a Shadow where Shaving should be.

"Well, it all goes on, and I suppose it all means something. But a baby is the Kingdom of God, and if you try to kiss a baby he will know whether you are shaved or not. Perhaps I am mixing up being shaved and being saved; my democratic sympathies have always led me to drop my 'h's.' In another moment I may suggest that goats represent the lost because goats have long beards. This is growing altogether too allegorical.

"Nevertheless," I added, as I paid the bill, "I have really been profoundly interested in what you told me about the New Shaving. Have you ever heard of a thing called the New theology?"

He smiled and said that he had not.

XXIII

The Toy Theatre

There is only one reason why all grown-up people do not play with toys; and it is a fair reason. The reason is that playing with toys takes so very much more time and trouble than anything else. Playing as children mean playing is the most serious thing in the world; and as soon as we have small duties or small sorrows we have to abandon to some extent so enormous and ambitious a plan of life. We have enough strength for politics and commerce and art and philosophy; we have not enough strength for play. This is a truth which every one will recognize who, as a child, has ever played with anything at all; any one who has played with bricks, any one who has played with dolls, any one who has played with tin soldiers. My journalistic work, which earns money, is not pursued with such awful persistency as that work which earned nothing.

Take the case of bricks. If you publish a book to-morrow in twelve volumes (it would be just like you) on "The Theory and Practice of European Architecture," your work may be laborious, but it is fundamentally frivolous. It is not serious as the work of a child piling one brick on the other is serious; for the simple reason that if your book is a bad book no one will ever be able ultimately and entirely to prove to you that it is a bad book. Whereas if his balance of bricks is a bad balance of bricks, it will simply tumble down. And if I know anything of children, he will set to work solemnly and sadly to build it up again. Whereas, if I know anything of authors, nothing would induce you to write your book again, or even to think of it again if you could help it.

Take the case of dolls. It is much easier to care for an educational cause than to care for a doll. It is as easy to write an article on education as to write an article on toffee or tramcars or anything else. But it is almost as difficult to look after a doll as to look after a child. The little girls that I meet in the little streets of Battersea worship their dolls in a way that reminds one not so much of play as idolatry. In some cases the love and care of the artistic symbol has actually become more important than the human reality which it was, I suppose, originally meant to symbolize.

I remember a Battersea little girl who wheeled her large baby sister stuffed into a doll's perambulator. When questioned on this course of conduct, she replied: "I haven't got a dolly, and Baby is pretending to be my dolly." Nature was indeed imitating art. First a doll had been a substitute for a child; afterwards a child was a mere substitute for a doll. But that opens other matters; the point is here that such devotion takes up most of the brain and most of the life; much as if it were really the thing which it is supposed to symbolize. The point is that the man writing on motherhood is merely an educationalist; the child playing with a doll is a mother.

Take the case of soldiers. A man writing an article on military strategy is simply a man writing an article; a horrid sight. But a boy making a campaign with tin soldiers is like a General making a campaign with live soldiers. He must to the limit of his juvenile powers think about the thing; whereas the war correspondent need not think at all. I remember a war correspondent who remarked after the capture of Methuen: "This renewed activity on the part of Delarey is probably due to his being short of stores." The same military critic had mentioned a few paragraphs before that Delarey was being hard pressed by a column which was pursuing him under the command of Methuen. Methuen chased Delarey; and Delarey's activity was due to his being short of stores. Otherwise he would have stood quite still while he was chased. I run after Jones with a hatchet, and if he turns round and tries to get rid of me the only possible explanation is that he has a very small balance at his bankers. I cannot believe that any boy playing at soldiers would be as idiotic as this. But then any one playing at anything has to be serious. Whereas, as I have only too good reason to know, if you are writing an article you can say anything that comes into your head.

BROADLY, THEN, WHAT KEEPS ADULTS from joining in children's games is, generally speaking, not that they have no pleasure in them; it is simply that they have no leisure for them. It is that they cannot afford the expenditure of toil and time and consideration for so grand and grave a scheme. I have been myself attempting for some time past to complete a play in a small toy theatre, the sort of toy theatre that used to be called Penny Plain and Twopence Coloured; only that I drew and coloured the figures and scenes myself. Hence I was free from the degrading obligation of having to pay either a penny or twopence; I only had to pay a shilling a sheet for good cardboard and a shilling a box for bad water colours. The kind of miniature stage I mean is probably familiar to every one; it is never more than a development of the stage which Skelt made and Stevenson celebrated.

But though I have worked much harder at the toy theatre than I ever worked at any tale or article, I cannot finish it; the work seems too heavy for me. I have to break off and betake myself to lighter employments; such as the biographies of great men. The play of "St. George and the Dragon," over which I have burnt the midnight oil (you must colour the thing by lamplight because that is how it will be seen), still lacks most conspicuously, alas! two wings of the Sultan's Palace, and also some comprehensible and workable way of getting up the curtain.

All this gives me a feeling touching the real meaning of immortality. In this world we cannot have pure pleasure. This is partly because pure pleasure would be dangerous to us and to our neighbours. But it is partly because pure pleasure is a great deal too much trouble. If I am ever in any other and better world, I hope that I shall have enough time to play with nothing but toy theatres; and I hope that I shall have enough divine and superhuman energy to act at least one play in them without a hitch.

MEANWHILE THE PHILOSOPHY OF TOY theatres is worth any one's consideration. All the essential morals which modern men need to learn could be deduced from this toy. Artistically considered, it reminds us of the main principle of art, the principle which is in most danger of being forgotten in our time. I mean the fact that art consists of limitation; the fact that art is limitation. Art does not consist in expanding things. Art consists of cutting things down, as I cut down with a pair of scissors my very ugly figures of St. George and the Dragon. Plato, who liked definite ideas, would like my cardboard dragon; for though the creature has few other artistic merits he is at least dragonish. The modern philosopher, who likes infinity, is quite welcome to a sheet of the plain cardboard. The most artistic thing about the theatrical art is the fact that the spectator looks at the whole thing through a window. This is true even of theatres inferior to my own; even at the Court Theatre or His Majesty's you are looking through a window; an unusually large window. But the advantage of the small theatre exactly is that you are looking through a small window. Has not every one noticed how sweet and startling any landscape looks when seen through an arch? This strong, square shape, this shutting off of everything else is not only an assistance to beauty; it is the essential of beauty. The most beautiful part of every picture is the frame.

This especially is true of the toy theatre; that, by reducing the scale of events it can introduce much larger events. Because it is small it could easily represent the earthquake in Jamaica. Because it is small it could easily represent the Day of Judgment. Exactly in so far as it is limited, so far it could play easily with falling cities or with falling stars. Meanwhile the big theatres are obliged to be economical because they are big. When we have understood this fact we shall have understood something of the reason why the world has always been first inspired by small nationalities. The vast Greek philosophy could fit easier into the small city of Athens than into the immense Empire of Persia. In the narrow streets of Florence Dante felt that there was room for Purgatory and Heaven and Hell. He would have been stifled by the British Empire. Great empires are necessarily prosaic; for it is beyond human power to act a great poem upon so great a scale. You can only represent very big ideas in very small spaces. My toy theatre is as philosophical as the drama of Athens.

XXIV

A Tragedy of Twopence

My relations with the readers of this page have been long and pleasant, but—perhaps for that very reason—I feel that the time has come when I ought to confess the one great crime of my life. It happened a long time ago; but it is not uncommon for a belated burst of remorse to reveal such dark episodes long after they have occurred. It has nothing to do with the orgies of the Anti-Puritan League. That body is so offensively respectable that a newspaper, in describing it the other day, referred to my friend Mr. Edgar Jepson as Canon Edgar Jepson; and it is believed that similar titles are intended for all of us. No; it is not by the conduct of Archbishop Crane, of Dean Chesterton, of the Rev. James Douglas, of Monsignor Bland, and even of that fine and virile old ecclesiastic, Cardinal Nesbit, that I wish (or rather, am driven by my conscience) to make this declaration. The crime was committed in solitude and without accomplices. Alone I did it. Let me, with the characteristic thirst of penitents to get the worst of the confession over, state it first of all in its most dreadful and indefensible form. There is at the present moment in a town in Germany (unless he has died of rage on discovering his wrong), a restaurant-keeper to whom I still owe twopence. I last left his open-air restaurant knowing that I owed him twopence. I carried it away under his nose, despite the fact that the nose was a decidedly Jewish one. I have never paid him, and it is highly improbable that I ever shall. How did this villainy come to occur in a life which has been, generally speaking, deficient in the dexterity necessary for fraud? The story is as follows—and it has a moral, though there may not be room for that.

It is a fair general rule for those travelling on the Continent that the easiest way of talking in a foreign language is to talk philosophy. The most difficult kind of talking is to talk about common necessities. The reason is obvious. The names of common necessities vary completely with each nation and are generally somewhat odd and quaint. How, for instance, could a Frenchman suppose that a coalbox would be called a "scuttle"? If he has ever seen the word scuttle it has been in the Jingo Press, where the "policy of scuttle" is used whenever we give up something to a small Power like Liberals, instead of giving up everything to a great Power, like Imperialists. What Englishman in Germany would be poet enough to guess that the Germans call a glove a "hand-shoe." Nations name their necessities by nicknames, so to speak. They call their tubs and stools by quaint, elvish, and almost affectionate names, as if they were their own children! But any one can argue about abstract things in a foreign language who has ever got as far as Exercise IV in a primer. For as soon as he can put a sentence together at all he finds that the words used in abstract or philosophical discussions are almost the same in all nations. They are the same, for the simple reason that they all come from the things that were the roots of our common civilisation. From Christianity, from the Roman Empire, from the mediaeval Church, or the French Revolution. "Nation," "citizen," "religion," "philosophy," "authority," "the Republic," words like these are nearly the same in all the countries in which we travel. Restrain, therefore, your exuberant admiration for the young man who can argue with six French atheists when he first lands at Dieppe. Even I can do that. But very likely the same young man does not know the French for a shoe-horn. But to this generalisation there are three great exceptions. (1) In the case of countries that are not European at all, and have never had our civic conceptions, or the old Latin scholarship. I do not pretend that the Patagonian phrase for "citizenship" at once leaps to the mind, or that a Dyak's word for "the Republic" has been familiar to me from the nursery. (2) In the case of Germany, where, although the principle does apply to many words such as "nation" and "philosophy," it does not apply so generally, because Germany has had a special and deliberate policy of encouraging the purely German part of its language. (3) In the case where one does not know any of the language at all, as is generally the case with me.

Such at least was my situation on the dark day on which I committed my crime. Two of the exceptional conditions which I have mentioned were combined. I was walking about a German town, and I knew no German. I knew, however, two or three of those great and solemn words which hold our European civilisation together—one of which is "cigar." As it was a hot and dreamy day, I sat down at a table in a sort of beer-garden, and ordered a cigar and a pot of lager. I drank the lager, and paid for it. I smoked the cigar, forgot to pay for it, and walked away, gazing rapturously at the royal outline of the Taunus mountains. After about ten minutes, I suddenly remembered that I had not paid for the cigar. I went back to the place of refreshment, and put down the money. But the proprietor also had forgotten the cigar, and he merely said guttural things in a tone of query, asking me, I suppose, what I wanted. I said "cigar," and he gave me a cigar. I endeavoured while putting down the money to wave away the cigar with gestures of refusal. He thought that my rejection was of the nature of a condemnation of that particular cigar, and brought me another. I whirled my arms like a windmill, seeking to convey by the sweeping universality of my gesture that my rejection was a rejection of cigars in general, not of that particular article. He mistook this for the ordinary impatience of common men, and rushed forward, his hands filled with miscellaneous cigars, pressing them upon me. In desperation I tried other kinds of pantomime, but the more cigars I refused the more and more rare and precious cigars were brought out of the deeps and recesses of the establishment. I tried in vain to think of a way of conveying to him the fact that I had already had the cigar. I imitated the action of a citizen smoking, knocking off and throwing away a cigar. The watchful proprietor only thought I was rehearsing (as in an ecstasy of anticipation) the joys of the cigar he was going to give me. At last I retired baffled: he would not take the money and leave the cigars alone. So that this restaurant-keeper (in whose face a love of money shone like the sun at noonday) flatly and firmly refused to receive the twopence that I certainly owed him; and I took that twopence of his away with me and rioted on it for months. I hope that on the last day the angels will break the truth very gently to that unhappy man.

THIS IS THE TRUE AND exact account of the Great Cigar Fraud, and the moral of it is this—that civilisation is founded upon abstractions. The idea of debt is one which cannot be conveyed by physical motions at all, because it is an abstract idea. And civilisation obviously would be nothing without debt. So when hard-headed fellows who study scientific sociology (which does not exist) come and tell you that civilisation is material or indifferent to the abstract, just ask yourselves how many of the things that make up our Society, the Law, or the Stocks and Shares, or the National Debt, you would be able to convey with your face and your ten fingers by grinning and gesticulating to a German innkeeper.

XXV

A Cab Ride Across Country

S own somewhere far off in the shallow dales of Hertfordshire there lies a village of great beauty, and I doubt not of admirable virtue, but of eccentric and unbalanced literary taste, which asked the present writer to come down to it on Sunday afternoon and give an address.

Now it was very difficult to get down to it at all on Sunday afternoon, owing to the indescribable state into which our national laws and customs have fallen in connection with the seventh day. It is not Puritanism; it is simply anarchy. I should have some sympathy with the Jewish Sabbath, if it were a Jewish Sabbath, and that for three reasons; first, that religion is an intrinsically sympathetic thing; second, that I cannot conceive any religion worth calling a religion without a fixed and material observance; and third, that the particular observance of sitting still and doing no work is one that suits my temperament down to the ground.

But the absurdity of the modern English convention is that it does not let a man sit still; it only perpetually trips him up when it has forced him to walk about. Our Sabbatarianism does not forbid us to ask a man in Battersea to come and talk in Hertfordshire; it only prevents his getting there. I can understand that a deity might be worshipped with joys, with flowers, and fireworks in the old European style. I can understand that a deity might be worshipped with sorrows. But I cannot imagine any deity being worshipped with inconveniences. Let the good Moslem go to Mecca, or let him abide in his tent, according to his feelings for religious symbols. But surely Allah cannot see anything particularly dignified in his servant being misled by the time-table, finding that the old Mecca express is not running, missing his connection at Bagdad, or having to wait three hours in a small side station outside Damascus.

So it was with me on this occasion. I found there was no telegraph service at all to this place; I found there was only one weak thread of train-service. Now if this had been the authority of real English religion, I should have submitted to it at once. If I believed that the telegraph clerk could not send the telegram because he was at that moment rigid in an ecstasy of prayer, I should think all telegrams unimportant in comparison. If I could believe that railway porters when relieved from their duties rushed with passion to the nearest place of worship, I should say that all lectures and everything else ought to give way to such a consideration. I should not complain if the national faith forbade me to make any appointments of labour or self-expression on the Sabbath. But, as it is, it only tells me that I may very probably keep the Sabbath by not keeping the appointment.

But I must resume the real details of my tale. I found that there was only one train in the whole of that Sunday by which I could even get within several hours or several miles of the time or place. I therefore went to the telephone, which is one of my favourite toys, and down which I have shouted many valuable, but prematurely arrested, monologues upon art and morals. I remember a mild shock of surprise when I discovered that one could use the telephone on Sunday; I did not expect it to be cut off, but I expected it to buzz more than on ordinary days, to the advancement of our national religion. Through this instrument, in fewer words than usual, and with a comparative economy of epigram, I ordered a taxi-cab to take me to the railway station. I have not a word to say in general either against telephones or taxi-cabs; they seem to me two of the purest and most poetic of the creations of modern scientific civilisation. Unfortunately, when the taxi-cab started, it did exactly what modern scientific civilisation has done—it broke down. The result of this was that when I arrived at King's Cross my only train was gone; there was a Sabbath calm in the station, a calm in the eyes of the porters, and in my breast, if calm at all, if any calm, a calm despair.

There was not, however, very much calm of any sort in my breast on first making the discovery; and it was turned to blinding horror when I learnt that I could not even send a telegram to the organisers of the meeting. To leave my entertainers in the lurch was sufficiently exasperating; to leave them without any intimation was simply low. I reasoned with the official. I said: "Do you really mean to say that if my brother were dying and my mother in this place, I could not communicate with her?" He was a man of literal and laborious mind; he asked me if my brother was dying. I answered that he was in excellent and even offensive health, but that I was inquiring upon a question of principle. What would happen if England were invaded, or if I alone knew how to turn aside a comet or an earthquake. He waved away these hypotheses in the most irresponsible spirit, but he was quite certain that telegrams could not reach this particular village. Then something exploded in me; that element of the outrageous which is the mother of all adventures sprang up ungovernable, and I decided that I would not be a cad merely because some of my remote ancestors had been Calvinists. I would keep my appointment if I lost all my money and all my wits. I went out into the quiet London street, where my quiet London cab was still waiting for its fare in the cold misty morning. I placed myself comfortably in the London cab and told the London driver to drive me to the other end of Hertfordshire. And he did.

I SHALL NOT FORGET THAT drive. It was doubtful whether, even in a motor-cab, the thing was possible with any consideration for the driver, not to speak of some slight consideration for the people in the road. I urged the driver to eat and drink something before he started, but he said (with I know not what pride of profession or delicate sense of adventure) that he would rather do it when we arrived—if we ever did. I was by no means so delicate; I bought a varied selection of pork-pies at a little shop that was open (why was that shop open?—it is all a mystery), and ate them as we went along. The beginning was sombre and irritating. I was annoyed, not with people, but with things, like a baby; with the motor for breaking down and with Sunday for being Sunday. And the sight of the northern slums expanded and ennobled, but did not decrease, my gloom: Whitechapel has an Oriental gaudiness in its squalor; Battersea and Camberwell have an indescribable bustle of democracy; but the poor parts of North London. . . well, perhaps I saw them wrongly under that ashen morning and on that foolish errand.

It was one of those days which more than once this year broke the retreat of winter; a winter day that began too late to be spring. We were already clear of the obstructing crowds and quickening our pace through a borderland of market gardens and isolated public-houses, when the grey showed golden patches and a good light began to glitter on everything. The cab went quicker and quicker. The open land whirled wider and wider; but I did not lose my sense of being battled with and thwarted that I had felt in the thronged slums. Rather the feeling increased, because of the great difficulty of space and time. The faster went the car, the fiercer and thicker I felt the fight.

G.K. CHESTERTON

The whole landscape seemed charging at me—and just missing me. The tall, shining grass went by like showers of arrows; the very trees seemed like lances hurled at my heart, and shaving it by a hair's breadth. Across some vast, smooth valley I saw a beech-tree by the white road stand up little and defiant. It grew bigger and bigger with blinding rapidity. It charged me like a tilting knight, seemed to hack at my head, and pass by. Sometimes when we went round a curve of road, the effect was yet more awful. It seemed as if some tree or windmill swung round to smite like a boomerang. The sun by this time was a blazing fact; and I saw that all Nature is chivalrous and militant. We do wrong to seek peace in Nature; we should rather seek the nobler sort of war; and see all the trees as green banners.

I GAVE MY ADDRESS, ARRIVING just when everybody was deciding to leave. When my cab came reeling into the market-place they decided, with evident disappointment, to remain. Over the lecture I draw a veil. When I came back home I was called to the telephone, and a meek voice expressed regret for the failure of the motor-cab, and even said something about any reasonable payment. "Whom can I pay for my own superb experience? What is the usual charge for seeing the clouds shattered by the sun? What is the market price of a tree blue on the sky-line and then blinding white in the sun? Mention your price for that windmill that stood behind the hollyhocks in the garden. Let me pay you for. . ." Here it was, I think, that we were cut off.

XXVI

The Two Noises

For three days and three nights the sea had charged England as Napoleon charged her at Waterloo. The phrase is instinctive, because away to the last grey line of the sea there was only the look of galloping squadrons, impetuous, but with a common purpose. The sea came on like cavalry, and when it touched the shore it opened the blazing eyes and deafening tongues of the artillery. I saw the worst assault at night on a seaside parade where the sea smote on the doors of England with the hammers of earthquake, and a white smoke went up into the black heavens. There one could thoroughly realise what an awful thing a wave really is. I talk like other people about the rushing swiftness of a wave. But the horrible thing about a wave is its hideous slowness. It lifts its load of water laboriously: in that style at once slow and slippery in which a Titan might lift a load of rock and then let it slip at last to be shattered into shock of dust. In front of me that night the waves were not like water: they were like falling city walls. The breaker rose first as if it did not wish to attack the earth; it wished only to attack the stars. For a time it stood up in the air as naturally as a tower; then it went a little wrong in its outline, like a tower that might some day fall. When it fell it was as if a powder magazine blew up.

I have never seen such a sea. All the time there blew across the land one of those stiff and throttling winds that one can lean up against like a wall. One expected anything to be blown out of shape at any instant; the lamp-post to be snapped like a green stalk, the tree to be whirled away like a straw. I myself should certainly have been blown out of shape if I had possessed any shape to be blown out of; for I walked along the edge of the stone embankment above the black and battering sea and could not rid myself of the idea that it was an invasion of England. But as I walked along this edge I was somewhat surprised to find that as I neared a certain spot another noise mingled with the ceaseless cannonade of the sea.

Somewhere at the back, in some pleasure ground or casino or

G.K. CHESTERTON

place of entertainment, an undaunted brass band was playing against the cosmic uproar. I do not know what band it was. Judging from the boisterous British Imperialism of most of the airs it played, I should think it was a German band. But there was no doubt about its energy, and when I came quite close under it it really drowned the storm. It was playing such things as "Tommy Atkins" and "You Can Depend on Young Australia," and many others of which I do not know the words, but I should think they would be "John, Pat, and Mac, With the Union Jack," or that fine though unwritten poem, "Wait till the Bull Dog gets a bite of you." Now, I for one detest Imperialism, but I have a great deal of sympathy with Jingoism. And there seemed something so touching about this unbroken and innocent bragging under the brutal menace of Nature that it made, if I may so put it, two tunes in my mind. It is so obvious and so jolly to be optimistic about England, especially when you are an optimist—and an Englishman. But through all that glorious brass came the voice of the invasion, the undertone of that awful sea. I did a foolish thing. As I could not express my meaning in an article, I tried to express it in a poem—a bad one. You can call it what you like. It might be called "Doubt," or "Brighton." It might be called "The Patriot," or yet again "The German Band." I would call it "The Two Voices," but that title has been taken for a grossly inferior poem. This is how it began—

> "They say the sun is on your knees
> A lamp to light your lands from harm,
> They say you turn the seven seas
> To little brooks about your farm.
> I hear the sea and the new song
> that calls you empress all day long.
>
> "(O fallen and fouled! O you that lie
> Dying in swamps—you shall not die,
> Your rich have secrets, and stronge lust,
> Your poor are chased about like dust,
> Emptied of anger and surprise—
> And God has gone out of their eyes,
> Your cohorts break—your captains lie,
> I say to you, you shall not die.)"

Then I revived a little, remembering that after all there is an English country that the Imperialists have never found. The British Empire may annex what it likes, it will never annex England. It has not even discovered the island, let alone conquered it. I took up the two tunes again with a greater sympathy for the first—

> *"I know the bright baptismal rains,*
> *I love your tender troubled skies,*
> *I know your little climbing lanes,*
> *Are peering into Paradise,*
> *From open hearth to orchard cool,*
> *How bountiful and beautiful.*
>
> *"(O throttled and without a cry,*
> *O strangled and stabbed, you shall not die,*
> *The frightful word is on your walls,*
> *The east sea to the west sea calls,*
> *The stars are dying in the sky,*
> *You shall not die; you shall not die.)"*

Then the two great noises grew deafening together, the noise of the peril of England and the louder noise of the placidity of England. It is their fault if the last verse was written a little rudely and at random—

> *"I see you how you smile in state*
> *Straight from the Peak to Plymouth Bar,*
> *You need not tell me you are great,*
> *I know how more than great you are.*
> *I know what William Shakespeare was,*
> *I have seen Gainsborough and the grass.*
>
> *"(O given to believe a lie,*
> *O my mad mother, do do not die,*
> *Whose eyes turn all ways but within,*
> *Whose sin is innocence of sin,*
> *Whose eyes, blinded with beams at noon,*
> *Can see the motes upon the moon,*
> *You shall your lover still pursue.*

G.K. CHESTERTON

To what last madhouse shelters you
I will uphold you, even I.
You that are dead. You shall not die.)"

But the sea would not stop for me any more than for Canute; and as for the German band, that would not stop for anybody.

XXVII

Some Policemen and a Moral

The other day I was nearly arrested by two excited policemen in a wood in Yorkshire. I was on a holiday, and was engaged in that rich and intricate mass of pleasures, duties, and discoveries which for the keeping off of the profane, we disguise by the exoteric name of Nothing. At the moment in question I was throwing a big Swedish knife at a tree, practising (alas, without success) that useful trick of knife-throwing by which men murder each other in Stevenson's romances.

Suddenly the forest was full of two policemen; there was something about their appearance in and relation to the greenwood that reminded me, I know not how, of some happy Elizabethan comedy. They asked what the knife was, who I was, why I was throwing it, what my address was, trade, religion, opinions on the Japanese war, name of favourite cat, and so on. They also said I was damaging the tree; which was, I am sorry to say, not true, because I could not hit it. The peculiar philosophical importance, however, of the incident was this. After some half-hour's animated conversation, the exhibition of an envelope, an unfinished poem, which was read with great care, and, I trust, with some profit, and one or two other subtle detective strokes, the elder of the two knights became convinced that I really was what I professed to be, that I was a journalist, that I was on the Daily News (this was the real stroke; they were shaken with a terror common to all tyrants), that I lived in a particular place as stated, and that I was stopping with particular people in Yorkshire, who happened to be wealthy and well-known in the neighbourhood.

In fact the leading constable became so genial and complimentary at last that he ended up by representing himself as a reader of my work. And when that was said, everything was settled. They acquitted me and let me pass.

"But," I said, "what of this mangled tree? It was to the rescue of that Dryad, tethered to the earth, that you rushed like knight-errants. You, the higher humanitarians, are not deceived by the seeming stillness of the green things, a stillness like the stillness of the cataract, a headlong and crashing silence. You know that a tree is but a creature tied to the ground by one leg. You will not let assassins with their Swedish daggers shed the green blood of such a being. But if so, why am I not in custody; where are my gyves? Produce, from some portion of your persons, my mouldy straw and my grated window. The facts of which I have just convinced you, that my name is Chesterton, that I am a journalist, that I am living with the well-known and philanthropic Mr. Blank of Ilkley, cannot have anything to do with the question of whether I have been guilty of cruelty to vegetables. The tree is none the less damaged even though it may reflect with a dark pride that it was wounded by a gentleman connected with the Liberal press. Wounds in the bark do not more rapidly close up because they are inflicted by people who are stopping with Mr. Blank of Ilkley. That tree, the ruin of its former self, the wreck of what was once a giant of the forest, now splintered and laid low by the brute superiority of a Swedish knife, that tragedy, constable, cannot be wiped out even by stopping for several months more with some wealthy person. It is incredible that you have no legal claim to arrest even the most august and fashionable persons on this charge. For if so, why did you interfere with me at all?"

I made the later and larger part of this speech to the silent wood, for the two policemen had vanished almost as quickly as they came. It is very possible, of course, that they were fairies. In that case the somewhat illogical character of their view of crime, law, and personal responsibility would find a bright and elfish explanation; perhaps if I had lingered in the glade till moonrise I might have seen rings of tiny policemen dancing on the sward; or running about with glow-worm belts, arresting grasshoppers for damaging blades of grass. But taking the bolder hypothesis, that they really were policemen, I find myself in a certain difficulty. I was certainly accused of something which was either an offence or was not. I was let off because I proved I was a guest at a big house. The inference seems painfully clear; either it is not a proof of infamy to throw a knife about in a lonely wood, or else it is a proof of innocence to know a rich man. Suppose a very poor person, poorer even than a journalist, a navvy or unskilled labourer, tramping in search of work, often changing his lodgings, often, perhaps, failing in his rent. Suppose he had been intoxicated with the green gaiety of the ancient wood. Suppose he had thrown knives at trees and could give no description of a dwelling-place except that he had been fired out of the last. As I walked home through a cloudy and purple twilight I wondered how he would have got on.

Moral. We English are always boasting that we are very illogical; there is no great harm in that. There is no subtle spiritual evil in the fact that people always brag about their vices; it is when they begin to brag about their virtues that they become insufferable. But there is this to be said, that illogicality in your constitution or your legal methods may become very dangerous if there happens to be some great national vice or national temptation which many take advantage of the chaos. Similarly, a drunkard ought to have strict rules and hours; a temperate man may obey his instincts.

Take some absurd anomaly in the British law—the fact, for instance, that a man ceasing to be an M. P. has to become Steward of the Chiltern Hundreds, an office which I believe was intended originally to keep down some wild robbers near Chiltern, wherever that is. Obviously this kind of illogicality does not matter very much, for the simple reason that there is no great temptation to take advantage of it. Men retiring from Parliament do not have any furious impulse to hunt robbers in the hills. But if there were a real danger that wise, white-haired, venerable politicians taking leave of public life would desire to do this (if, for instance, there were any money in it), then clearly, if we went on saying that the illogicality did not matter, when (as a matter of fact) Sir Michael Hicks-Beach was hanging Chiltern shop-keepers every day and taking their property, we should be very silly. The illogicality would matter, for it would have become an excuse for indulgence. It is only the very good who can live riotous lives.

Now this is exactly what is present in cases of police investigation such as the one narrated above. There enters into such things a great national sin, a far greater sin than drink—the habit of respecting a gentleman. Snobbishness has, like drink, a kind of grand poetry. And snobbishness has this peculiar and devilish quality of evil, that it is rampant among very kindly people, with open hearts and houses. But it is our great English vice; to be watched more fiercely than small-pox. If a man wished to hear the worst and wickedest thing in England summed up in casual English words, he would not find it in any foul oaths or ribald quarrelling. He would find it in the fact that the best kind of working man, when he wishes to praise any one, calls him "a gentleman." It never occurs to him that he might as well call him "a marquis," or "a privy councillor"—that he is simply naming a rank or class, not a phrase for a good man. And this perennial temptation to a shameful admiration, must, and, I think, does, constantly come in and distort and poison our police methods.

In this case we must be logical and exact; for we have to keep watch upon ourselves. The power of wealth, and that power at its vilest, is increasing in the modern world. A very good and just people, without this temptation, might not need, perhaps, to make clear rules and systems to guard themselves against the power of our great financiers. But that is because a very just people would have shot them long ago, from mere native good feeling.

XXVIII

THE LION

In the town of Belfort I take a chair and I sit down in the street. We talk in a cant phrase of the Man in the Street, but the Frenchman is the man in the street. Things quite central for him are connected with these lamp-posts and pavements; everything from his meals to his martyrdoms. When first an Englishman looks at a French town or village his first feeling is simply that it is uglier than an English town or village; when he looks again he sees that this comparative absence of the picturesque is chiefly expressed in the plain, precipitous frontage of the houses standing up hard and flat out of the street like the cardboard houses in a pantomime—a hard angularity allied perhaps to the harshness of French logic. When he looks a third time he sees quite simply that it is all because the houses have no front gardens. The vague English spirit loves to have the entrance to its house softened by bushes and broken by steps. It likes to have a little anteroom of hedges half in the house and half out of it; a green room in a double sense. The Frenchman desires no such little pathetic ramparts or halting places, for the street itself is a thing natural and familiar to him.

THE FRENCH HAVE NO FRONT gardens; but the street is every man's front garden. There are trees in the street, and sometimes fountains. The street is the Frenchman's tavern, for he drinks in the street. It is his dining-room, for he dines in the street. It is his British Museum, for the statues and monuments in French streets are not, as with us, of the worst, but of the best, art of the country, and they are often actually as historical as the Pyramids. The street again is the Frenchman's Parliament, for France has never taken its Chamber of Deputies so seriously as we take our House of Commons, and the quibbles of mere elected nonentities in an official room seem feeble to a people whose fathers have heard the voice of Desmoulins like a trumpet under open heaven, or Victor Hugo shouting from his carriage amid the wreck of the second Republic. And as the Frenchman drinks in the street and dines in the street so also he fights in the street and dies in the street, so that the street can never be commonplace to him.

Take, for instance, such a simple object as a lamp-post. In London a lamp-post is a comic thing. We think of the intoxicated gentleman embracing it, and recalling ancient friendship. But in Paris a lamp-post is a tragic thing. For we think of tyrants hanged on it, and of an end of the world. There is, or was, a bitter Republican paper in Paris called LA LANTERNE. How funny it would be if there were a Progressive paper in England called THE LAMP POST! We have said, then, that the Frenchman is the man in the street; that he can dine in the street, and die in the street. And if I ever pass through Paris and find him going to bed in the street, I shall say that he is still true to the genius of his civilisation. All that is good and all that is evil in France is alike connected with this open-air element. French democracy and French indecency are alike part of the desire to have everything out of doors. Compared to a café, a public-house is a private house.

THERE WERE TWO REASONS WHY all these fancies should float through the mind in the streets of this especial town of Belfort. First of all, it lies close upon the boundary of France and Germany, and boundaries are the most beautiful things in the world. To love anything is to love its boundaries; thus children will always play on the edge of anything. They build castles on the edge of the sea, and can only be restrained by public proclamation and private violence from walking on the edge of the grass. For when we have come to the end of a thing we have come to the beginning of it.

Hence this town seemed all the more French for being on the very margin of Germany, and although there were many German touches in the place—German names, larger pots of beer, and enormous theatrical barmaids dressed up in outrageous imitation of Alsatian peasants—yet the fixed French colour seemed all the stronger for these specks of something else. All day long and all night long troops of dusty, swarthy, scornful little soldiers went plodding through the streets with an air of stubborn disgust, for German soldiers look as if they despised you, but French soldiers as if they despised you and themselves even more than you. It is a part, I suppose, of the realism of the nation which has made it good at war and science and other things in which what is necessary is combined with what is nasty. And the soldiers and the civilians alike had most of them cropped hair, and that curious kind of head which to an Englishman looks almost brutal, the kind that we call a bullet-head. Indeed, we are speaking very appropriately when we call it a bullet-head, for in intellectual history the heads of Frenchmen have been bullets—yes, and explosive bullets.

BUT THERE WAS A SECOND reason why in this place one should think particularly of the open-air politics and the open-air art of the French. For this town of Belfort is famous for one of the most typical and powerful of the public monuments of France. From the café table at which I sit I can see the hill beyond the town on which hangs the high and flat-faced citadel, pierced with many windows, and warmed in the evening light. On the steep hill below it is a huge stone lion, itself as large as a hill. It is hacked out of the rock with a sort of gigantic impression. No trivial attempt has been made to make it like a common statue; no attempt to carve the mane into curls, or to distinguish the monster minutely from the earth out of which he rises, shaking the world. The face of the lion has something of the bold conventionality of Assyrian art. The mane of the lion is left like a shapeless cloud of tempest, as if it might literally be said of him that God had clothed his neck with thunder. Even at this distance the thing looks vast, and in some sense prehistoric. Yet it was carved only a little while ago. It commemorates the fact that this town was never taken by the Germans through all the terrible year, but only laid down its arms at last at the command of its own Government. But the spirit of it has been in this land from the beginning—the spirit of something defiant and almost defeated.

As I leave this place and take the railway into Germany the news comes thicker and thicker up the streets that Southern France is in a flame, and that there perhaps will be fought out finally the awful modern battle of the rich and poor. And as I pass into quieter places for the last sign of France on the sky-line, I see the Lion of Belfort stand at bay, the last sight of that great people which has never been at peace.

XXIX

HUMANITY: AN INTERLUDE

E xcept for some fine works of art, which seem to be there by accident, the City of Brussels is like a bad Paris, a Paris with everything noble cut out, and everything nasty left in. No one can understand Paris and its history who does not understand that its fierceness is the balance and justification of its frivolity. It is called a city of pleasure; but it may also very specially be called a city of pain. The crown of roses is also a crown of thorns. Its people are too prone to hurt others, but quite ready also to hurt themselves. They are martyrs for religion, they are martyrs for irreligion; they are even martyrs for immorality. For the indecency of many of their books and papers is not of the sort which charms and seduces, but of the sort that horrifies and hurts; they are torturing themselves. They lash their own patriotism into life with the same whips which most men use to lash foreigners to silence. The enemies of France can never give an account of her infamy or decay which does not seem insipid and even polite compared with the things which the Nationalists of France say about their own nation. They taunt and torment themselves; sometimes they even deliberately oppress themselves. Thus, when the mob of Paris could make a Government to please itself, it made a sort of sublime tyranny to order itself about. The spirit is the same from the Crusades or St. Bartholomew to the apotheosis of Zola. The old religionists tortured men physically for a moral truth. The new realists torture men morally for a physical truth.

Now Brussels is Paris without this constant purification of pain. Its indecencies are not regrettable incidents in an everlasting revolution. It has none of the things which make good Frenchmen love Paris; it has only the things which make unspeakable Englishmen love it. It has the part which is cosmopolitan—and narrows; not the part which is Parisian—and universal. You can find there (as commonly happens in modern centres) the worst things of all nations—the DAILY MAIL from England, the cheap philosophies from Germany, the loose novels of France, and the drinks of America. But there is no English broad fun, no German kindly ceremony, no American exhilaration, and, above all, no French tradition of fighting for an idea. Though all the boulevards look like Parisian boulevards, though all the shops look like Parisian shops, you cannot look at them steadily for two minutes without feeling the full distance between, let us say, King Leopold and fighters like Clemenceau and Deroulède.

FOR ALL THESE REASONS, AND many more, when I had got into Brussels I began to make all necessary arrangements for getting out of it again; and I had impulsively got into a tram which seemed to be going out of the city. In this tram there were two men talking; one was a little man with a black French beard; the other was a baldish man with bushy whiskers, like the financial foreign count in a three-act farce. And about the time that we reached the suburb of the city, and the traffic grew thinner, and the noises more few, I began to hear what they were saying. Though they spoke French quickly, their words were fairly easy to follow, because they were all long words. Anybody can understand long words because they have in them all the lucidity of Latin.

The man with the black beard said: "It must that we have the Progress."

The man with the whiskers parried this smartly by saying: "It must also that we have the Consolidation International."

This is a sort of discussion which I like myself, so I listened with some care, and I think I picked up the thread of it. One of the Belgians was a Little Belgian, as we speak of a Little Englander. The other was a Belgian Imperialist, for though Belgium is not quite strong enough to be altogether a nation, she is quite strong enough to be an empire. Being a nation means standing up to your equals, whereas being an empire only means kicking your inferiors. The man with whiskers was the Imperialist, and he was saying: "The science, behold there the new guide of humanity."

And the man with the beard answered him: "It does not suffice to have progress in the science; one must have it also in the sentiment of the human justice."

This remark I applauded, as if at a public meeting, but they were much too keen on their argument to hear me. The views I have often heard in England, but never uttered so lucidly, and certainly never so fast. Though Belgian by nation they must both have been essentially French. Whiskers was great on education, which, it seems, is on the march. All the world goes to make itself instructed. It must that the more instructed enlighten the less instructed. Eh, well then, the

European must impose upon the savage the science and the light. Also (apparently) he must impose himself on the savage while he is about it. To-day one travelled quickly. The science had changed all. For our fathers, they were religious, and (what was worse) dead. To-day humanity had electricity to the hand; the machines came from triumphing; all the lines and limits of the globe effaced themselves. Soon there would not be but the great Empires and confederations, guided by the science, always the science.

Here Whiskers stopped an instant for breath; and the man with the sentiment for human justice had "la parole" off him in a flash. Without doubt Humanity was on the march, but towards the sentiments, the ideal, the methods moral and pacific. Humanity directed itself towards Humanity. For your wars and empires on behalf of civilisation, what were they in effect? The war, was it not itself an affair of the barbarism? The Empires were they not things savage? The Humanity had passed all that; she was now intellectual. Tolstoy had refined all human souls with the sentiments the most delicate and just. Man was become a spirit; the wings pushed. . .

At this important point of evolution the tram came to a jerky stoppage; and staring around I found, to my stunned consternation, that it was almost dark, that I was far away from Brussels, that I could not dream of getting back to dinner; in short, that through the clinging fascination of this great controversy on Humanity and its recent complete alteration by science or Tolstoy, I had landed myself Heaven knows where. I dropped hastily from the suburban tram and let it go on without me.

I was alone in the flat fields out of sight of the city. On one side of the road was one of those small, thin woods which are common in all countries, but of which, by a coincidence, the mystical painters of Flanders were very fond. The night was closing in with cloudy purple and grey; there was one ribbon of silver, the last rag of the sunset. Through the wood went one little path, and somehow it suggested that it might lead to some sign of life—there was no other sign of life on the horizon. I went along it, and soon sank into a sort of dancing twilight of all those tiny trees. There is something subtle and bewildering about that sort of frail and fantastic wood. A forest of big trees seems like a bodily barrier; but somehow that mist of thin lines seems like a spiritual barrier. It is as if one were caught in a fairy cloud or could not pass a phantom. When I had well lost the last gleam of the high road a curious and definite feeling came upon me. Now I suddenly felt something much more practical and extraordinary—the absence of humanity: inhuman loneliness. Of course, there was nothing really lost in my state; but the mood may hit one anywhere. I wanted men—any men; and I felt our awful alliance over all the globe. And at last, when I had walked for what seemed a long time, I saw a light too near the earth to mean anything except the image of God.

I came out on a clear space and a low, long cottage, the door of which was open, but was blocked by a big grey horse, who seemed to prefer to eat with his head inside the sitting-room. I got past him, and found he was being fed by a young man who was sitting down and drinking beer inside, and who saluted me with heavy rustic courtesy, but in a strange tongue. The room was full of staring faces like owls, and these I traced at length as belonging to about six small children. Their father was still working in the fields, but their mother rose when I entered. She smiled, but she and all the rest spoke some rude language, Flamand, I suppose; so that we had to be kind to each other by signs. She fetched me beer, and pointed out my way with her finger; and I drew a picture to please the children; and as it was a picture of two men hitting each other with swords, it pleased them very much. Then I gave a Belgian penny to each child, for as I said on chance in French, "It must be that we have the economic equality." But they had never heard of economic equality, while all Battersea workmen have heard of economic equality, though it is true that they haven't got it.

I found my way back to the city, and some time afterwards I actually saw in the street my two men talking, no doubt still saying, one that Science had changed all in Humanity, and the other that Humanity was now pushing the wings of the purely intellectual. But for me Humanity was hooked on to an accidental picture. I thought of a low and lonely house in the flats, behind a veil or film of slight trees, a man breaking the ground as men have broken from the first morning, and a huge grey horse champing his food within a foot of a child's head, as in the stable where Christ was born.

XXX

The Little Birds Who Won't Sing

O n my last morning on the Flemish coast, when I knew that in a few hours I should be in England, my eye fell upon one of the details of Gothic carving of which Flanders is full. I do not know whether the thing is old, though it was certainly knocked about and indecipherable, but at least it was certainly in the style and tradition of the early Middle Ages. It seemed to represent men bending themselves (not to say twisting themselves) to certain primary employments. Some seemed to be sailors tugging at ropes; others, I think, were reaping; others were energetically pouring something into something else. This is entirely characteristic of the pictures and carvings of the early thirteenth century, perhaps the most purely vigorous time in all history. The great Greeks preferred to carve their gods and heroes doing nothing. Splendid and philosophic as their composure is there is always about it something that marks the master of many slaves. But if there was one thing the early mediaevals liked it was representing people doing something—hunting or hawking, or rowing boats, or treading grapes, or making shoes, or cooking something in a pot. "Quicquid agunt homines, votum, timor, ira voluptas." (I quote from memory.) The Middle Ages is full of that spirit in all its monuments and manuscripts. Chaucer retains it in his jolly insistence on everybody's type of trade and toil. It was the earliest and youngest resurrection of Europe, the time when social order was strengthening, but had not yet become oppressive; the time when religious faiths were strong, but had not yet been exasperated. For this reason the whole effect of Greek and Gothic carving is different. The figures in the Elgin marbles, though often reining their steeds for an instant in the air, seem frozen for ever at that perfect instant. But a mass of mediaeval carving seems actually a sort of bustle or hubbub in stone. Sometimes one cannot help feeling that the groups actually move and mix, and the whole front of a great cathedral has the hum of a huge hive.

But about these particular figures there was a peculiarity of which I could not be sure. Those of them that had any heads had very curious heads, and it seemed to me that they had their mouths open. Whether or no this really meant anything or was an accident of nascent art I do not know; but in the course of wondering I recalled to my mind the fact that singing was connected with many of the tasks there suggested, that there were songs for reapers and songs for sailors hauling ropes. I was still thinking about this small problem when I walked along the pier at Ostend; and I heard some sailors uttering a measured shout as they laboured, and I remembered that sailors still sing in chorus while they work, and even sing different songs according to what part of their work they are doing. And a little while afterwards, when my sea journey was over, the sight of men working in the English fields reminded me again that there are still songs for harvest and for many agricultural routines. And I suddenly wondered why if this were so it should be quite unknown, for any modern trade to have a ritual poetry. How did people come to chant rude poems while pulling certain ropes or gathering certain fruit, and why did nobody do anything of the kind while producing any of the modern things? Why is a modern newspaper never printed by people singing in chorus? Why do shopmen seldom, if ever, sing?

If reapers sing while reaping, why should not auditors sing while auditing and bankers while banking? If there are songs for all the separate things that have to be done in a boat, why are there not songs for all the separate things that have to be done in a bank? As the train from Dover flew through the Kentish gardens, I tried to write a few songs suitable for commercial gentlemen. Thus, the work of bank clerks when casting up columns might begin with a thundering chorus in praise of Simple Addition.

"Up my lads and lift the ledgers, sleep and ease are o'er. Hear the Stars of Morning shouting: 'Two and Two are four.' Though the creeds and realms are reeling, though the sophists roar, Though we weep and pawn our watches, Two and Two are Four."

"There's a run upon the Bank—Stand away! For the Manager's a crank and the Secretary drank, and the

Upper Tooting Bank
Turns to bay!
Stand close: there is a run
On the Bank.
Of our ship, our royal one, let the ringing legend run,

That she fired with every gun
Ere she sank."

AND AS I CAME INTO the cloud of London I met a friend of mine who actually is in a bank, and submitted these suggestions in rhyme to him for use among his colleagues. But he was not very hopeful about the matter. It was not (he assured me) that he underrated the verses, or in any sense lamented their lack of polish. No; it was rather, he felt, an indefinable something in the very atmosphere of the society in which we live that makes it spiritually difficult to sing in banks. And I think he must be right; though the matter is very mysterious. I may observe here that I think there must be some mistake in the calculations of the Socialists. They put down all our distress, not to a moral tone, but to the chaos of private enterprise. Now, banks are private; but post-offices are Socialistic: therefore I naturally expected that the post-office would fall into the collectivist idea of a chorus. Judge of my surprise when the lady in my local post-office (whom I urged to sing) dismissed the idea with far more coldness than the bank clerk had done. She seemed indeed, to be in a considerably greater state of depression than he. Should any one suppose that this was the effect of the verses themselves, it is only fair to say that the specimen verse of the Post-Office Hymn ran thus:

"O'er London our letters are shaken like snow,
Our wires o'er the world like the thunderbolts go.
The news that may marry a maiden in Sark,
Or kill an old lady in Finsbury Park."

Chorus (with a swing of joy and energy):

"Or kill an old lady in Finsbury Park."

And the more I thought about the matter the more painfully certain it seemed that the most important and typical modern things could not be done with a chorus. One could not, for instance, be a great financier and sing; because the essence of being a great financier is that you keep quiet. You could not even in many modern circles be a public man and sing; because in those circles the essence of being a public man is that you do nearly everything in private. Nobody would imagine a chorus of money-lenders. Every one knows the story of the solicitors' corps of volunteers who, when the Colonel on the battlefield cried "Charge!" all said simultaneously, "Six-and-eightpence." Men can sing while charging in a military, but hardly in a legal sense. And at the end of my reflections I had really got no further than the sub-conscious feeling of my friend the bank-clerk—that there is something spiritually suffocating about our life; not about our laws merely, but about our life. Bank-clerks are without songs, not because they are poor, but because they are sad. Sailors are much poorer. As I passed homewards I passed a little tin building of some religious sort, which was shaken with shouting as a trumpet is torn with its own tongue. THEY were singing anyhow; and I had for an instant a fancy I had often had before: that with us the super-human is the only place where you can find the human. Human nature is hunted and has fled into sanctuary.

XXXI

THE RIDDLE OF THE IVY

More than a month ago, when I was leaving London for a holiday, a friend walked into my flat in Battersea and found me surrounded with half-packed luggage.

"You seem to be off on your travels," he said. "Where are you going?"

With a strap between my teeth I replied, "To Battersea."

"The wit of your remark," he said, "wholly escapes me."

"I am going to Battersea," I repeated, "to Battersea viâ Paris, Belfort, Heidelberg, and Frankfort. My remark contained no wit. It contained simply the truth. I am going to wander over the whole world until once more I find Battersea. Somewhere in the seas of sunset or of sunrise, somewhere in the ultimate archipelago of the earth, there is one little island which I wish to find: an island with low green hills and great white cliffs. Travellers tell me that it is called England (Scotch travellers tell me that it is called Britain), and there is a rumour that somewhere in the heart of it there is a beautiful place called Battersea."

"I suppose it is unnecessary to tell you," said my friend, with an air of intellectual comparison, "that this is Battersea?"

"It is quite unnecessary," I said, "and it is spiritually untrue. I cannot see any Battersea here; I cannot see any London or any England. I cannot see that door. I cannot see that chair: because a cloud of sleep and custom has come across my eyes. The only way to get back to them is to go somewhere else; and that is the real object of travel and the real pleasure of holidays. Do you suppose that I go to France in order to see France? Do you suppose that I go to Germany in order to see Germany? I shall enjoy them both; but it is not them that I am seeking. I am seeking Battersea. The whole object of travel is not to set foot on foreign land; it is at last to set foot on one's own country as a foreign land. Now I warn you that this Gladstone bag is compact and heavy, and that if you utter that word 'paradox' I shall hurl it at your head. I did not make the world, and I did not make it paradoxical. It is not my fault, it is the truth, that the only way to go to England is to go away from it."

But when, after only a month's travelling, I did come back to England, I was startled to find that I had told the exact truth.

England did break on me at once beautifully new and beautifully old. To land at Dover is the right way to approach England (most things that are hackneyed are right), for then you see first the full, soft gardens of Kent, which are, perhaps, an exaggeration, but still a typical exaggeration, of the rich rusticity of England. As it happened, also, a fellow-traveller with whom I had fallen into conversation felt the same freshness, though for another cause. She was an American lady who had seen Europe, and had never yet seen England, and she expressed her enthusiasm in that simple and splendid way which is natural to Americans, who are the most idealistic people in the whole world. Their only danger is that the idealist can easily become the idolator. And the American has become so idealistic that he even idealises money. But (to quote a very able writer of American short stories) that is another story.

"I have never been in England before," said the American lady, "yet it is so pretty that I feel as if I have been away from it for a long time."

"So you have," I said; "you have been away for three hundred years."

"What a lot of ivy you have," she said. "It covers the churches and it buries the houses. We have ivy; but I have never seen it grow like that."

"I am interested to hear it," I replied, "for I am making a little list of all the things that are really better in England. Even a month on the Continent, combined with intelligence, will teach you that there are many things that are better abroad. All the things that the DAILY MAIL calls English are better abroad. But there are things entirely English and entirely good. Kippers, for instance, and Free Trade, and front gardens, and individual liberty, and the Elizabethan drama, and hansom cabs, and cricket, and Mr. Will Crooks. Above all, there is the happy and holy custom of eating a heavy breakfast. I cannot imagine that Shakespeare began the day with rolls and coffee, like a Frenchman or a German. Surely he began with bacon or bloaters. In fact, a light bursts upon me; for the first time I see the real meaning of Mrs. Gallup and the Great Cipher. It is merely a mistake in the matter of a capital letter. I withdraw my objections; I accept everything; bacon did write Shakespeare."

"I cannot look at anything but the ivy," she said, "it looks so comfortable."

While she looked at the ivy I opened for the first time for many weeks an English newspaper, and I read a speech of Mr. Balfour in which he said that the House of Lords ought to be preserved because it represented something in the nature of permanent public opinion of England, above the ebb and flow of the parties. Now Mr. Balfour is a perfectly sincere patriot, a man who, from his own point of view, thinks long and seriously about the public needs, and he is, moreover, a man of entirely exceptionable intellectual power. But alas, in spite of all this, when I had read that speech I thought with a heavy heart that there was one more thing that I had to add to the list of the specially English things, such as kippers and cricket; I had to add the specially English kind of humbug. In France things are attacked and defended for what they are. The Catholic Church is attacked because it is Catholic, and defended because it is Catholic. The Republic is defended because it is Republican, and attacked because it is Republican. But here is the ablest of English politicians consoling everybody by telling them that the House of Lords is not really the House of Lords, but something quite different, that the foolish accidental peers whom he meets every night are in some mysterious way experts upon the psychology of the democracy; that if you want to know what the very poor want you must ask the very rich, and that if you want the truth about Hoxton, you must ask for it at Hatfield. If the Conservative defender of the House of Lords were a logical French politician he would simply be a liar. But being an English politician he is simply a poet. The English love of believing that all is as it should be, the English optimism combined with the strong English imagination, is too much even for the obvious facts. In a cold, scientific sense, of course, Mr. Balfour knows that nearly all the Lords who are not Lords by accident are Lords by bribery. He knows, and (as Mr. Belloc excellently said) everybody in Parliament knows the very names of the peers who have purchased their peerages. But the glamour of comfort, the pleasure of reassuring himself and reassuring others, is too strong for this original knowledge; at last it fades from him, and he sincerely and earnestly calls on Englishmen to join with him in admiring an august and public-spirited Senate, having wholly forgotten that the Senate really consists of idiots whom he has himself despised; and adventurers whom he has himself ennobled.

"Your ivy is so beautifully soft and thick," said the American lady, "it seems to cover almost everything. It must be the most poetical thing in England."

"It is very beautiful," I said, "and, as you say, it is very English. Charles Dickens, who was almost more English than England, wrote one of his rare poems about the beauty of ivy. Yes, by all means let us admire the ivy, so deep, so warm, so full of a genial gloom and a grotesque tenderness. Let us admire the ivy; and let us pray to God in His mercy that it may not kill the tree."

XXXII

The Travellers in State

The other day, to my great astonishment, I caught a train; it was a train going into the Eastern Counties, and I only just caught it. And while I was running along the train (amid general admiration) I noticed that there were a quite peculiar and unusual number of carriages marked "Engaged." On five, six, seven, eight, nine carriages was pasted the little notice: at five, six, seven, eight, nine windows were big bland men staring out in the conscious pride of possession. Their bodies seemed more than usually impenetrable, their faces more than usual placid. It could not be the Derby, if only for the minor reasons that it was the opposite direction and the wrong day. It could hardly be the King. It could hardly be the French President. For, though these distinguished persons naturally like to be private for three hours, they are at least public for three minutes. A crowd can gather to see them step into the train; and there was no crowd here, or any police ceremonial.

Who were those awful persons, who occupied more of the train than a bricklayer's beanfeast, and yet were more fastidious and delicate than the King's own suite? Who were these that were larger than a mob, yet more mysterious than a monarch? Was it possible that instead of our Royal House visiting the Tsar, he was really visiting us? Or does the House of Lords have a breakfast? I waited and wondered until the train slowed down at some station in the direction of Cambridge. Then the large, impenetrable men got out, and after them got out the distinguished holders of the engaged seats. They were all dressed decorously in one colour; they had neatly cropped hair; and they were chained together.

I looked across the carriage at its only other occupant, and our eyes met. He was a small, tired-looking man, and, as I afterwards learnt, a native of Cambridge; by the look of him, some working tradesman there, such as a journeyman tailor or a small clock-mender. In order to make conversation I said I wondered where the convicts were going. His mouth twitched with the instinctive irony of our poor, and he said: "I don't s'pose they're goin' on an 'oliday at the seaside with little spades and pails." I was naturally delighted, and, pursuing the same vein of literary invention, I suggested that perhaps dons were taken down to Cambridge chained together like this. And as he lived in Cambridge, and had seen several dons, he was pleased with such a scheme. Then when we had ceased to laugh, we suddenly became quite silent; and the bleak, grey eyes of the little man grew sadder and emptier than an open sea. I knew what he was thinking, because I was thinking the same, because all modern sophists are only sophists, and there is such a thing as mankind. Then at last (and it fell in as exactly as the right last note of a tune one is trying to remember) he said: "Well, I s'pose we 'ave to do it." And in those three things, his first speech and his silence and his second speech, there were all the three great fundamental facts of the English democracy, its profound sense of humour, its profound sense of pathos, and its profound sense of helplessness.

IT CANNOT BE TOO OFTEN repeated that all real democracy is an attempt (like that of a jolly hostess) to bring the shy people out. For every practical purpose of a political state, for every practical purpose of a tea-party, he that abaseth himself must be exalted. At a tea-party it is equally obvious that he that exalteth himself must be abased, if possible without bodily violence. Now people talk of democracy as being coarse and turbulent: it is a self-evident error in mere history. Aristocracy is the thing that is always coarse and turbulent: for it means appealing to the self-confident people. Democracy means appealing to the different people. Democracy means getting those people to vote who would never have the cheek to govern: and (according to Christian ethics) the precise people who ought to govern are the people who have not the cheek to do it. There is a strong example of this truth in my friend in the train. The only two types we hear of in this argument about crime and punishment are two very rare and abnormal types.

We hear of the stark sentimentalist, who talks as if there were no problem at all: as if physical kindness would cure everything: as if one need only pat Nero and stroke Ivan the Terrible. This mere belief in bodily humanitarianism is not sentimental; it is simply snobbish. For if comfort gives men virtue, the comfortable classes ought to be virtuous—which is absurd. Then, again, we do hear of the yet weaker and more watery type of sentimentalists: I mean the sentimentalist who says, with a sort of splutter, "Flog the brutes!" or who tells you with innocent obscenity "what he would do" with a certain man—always supposing the man's hands were tied.

G.K. CHESTERTON

This is the more effeminate type of the two; but both are weak and unbalanced. And it is only these two types, the sentimental humanitarian and the sentimental brutalitarian, whom one hears in the modern babel. Yet you very rarely meet either of them in a train. You never meet anyone else in a controversy. The man you meet in a train is like this man that I met: he is emotionally decent, only he is intellectually doubtful. So far from luxuriating in the loathsome things that could be "done" to criminals, he feels bitterly how much better it would be if nothing need be done. But something must be done. "I s'pose we 'ave to do it." In short, he is simply a sane man, and of a sane man there is only one safe definition. He is a man who can have tragedy in his heart and comedy in his head.

Now the real difficulty of discussing decently this problem of the proper treatment of criminals is that both parties discuss the matter without any direct human feeling. The denouncers of wrong are as cold as the organisers of wrong. Humanitarianism is as hard as inhumanity.

Let me take one practical instance. I think the flogging arranged in our modern prisons is a filthy torture; all its scientific paraphernalia, the photographing, the medical attendance, prove that it goes to the last foul limit of the boot and rack. The cat is simply the rack without any of its intellectual reasons. Holding this view strongly, I open the ordinary humanitarian books or papers and I find a phrase like this, "The lash is a relic of barbarism." So is the plough. So is the fishing net. So is the horn or the staff or the fire lit in winter. What an inexpressibly feeble phrase for anything one wants to attack—a relic of barbarism! It is as if a man walked naked down the street to-morrow, and we said that his clothes were not quite in the latest fashion. There is nothing particularly nasty about being a relic of barbarism. Man is a relic of barbarism. Civilisation is a relic of barbarism.

But torture is not a relic of barbarism at all. In actuality it is simply a relic of sin; but in comparative history it may well be called a relic of civilisation. It has always been most artistic and elaborate when everything else was most artistic and elaborate. Thus it was detailed exquisite in the late Roman Empire, in the complex and gorgeous sixteenth century, in the centralised French monarchy a hundred years before the Revolution, and in the great Chinese civilisation to this day. This is, first and last, the frightful thing we must remember. In so far as we grow instructed and refined we are not (in any sense whatever) naturally moving away from torture. We may be moving towards torture. We must know what we are doing, if we are to avoid the enormous secret cruelty which has crowned every historic civilisation.

The train moves more swiftly through the sunny English fields. They have taken the prisoners away, and I do not know what they have done with them.

XXXIII

The Prehistoric Railway Station

A railway station is an admirable place, although Ruskin did not think so; he did not think so because he himself was even more modern than the railway station. He did not think so because he was himself feverish, irritable, and snorting like an engine. He could not value the ancient silence of the railway station.

"In a railway station," he said, "you are in a hurry, and therefore, miserable"; but you need not be either unless you are as modern as Ruskin. The true philosopher does not think of coming just in time for his train except as a bet or a joke.

The only way of catching a train I have ever discovered is to be late for the one before. Do this, and you will find in a railway station much of the quietude and consolation of a cathedral. It has many of the characteristics of a great ecclesiastical building; it has vast arches, void spaces, coloured lights, and, above all, it has recurrence or ritual. It is dedicated to the celebration of water and fire the two prime elements of all human ceremonial. Lastly, a station resembles the old religions rather than the new religions in this point, that people go there. In connection with this it should also be remembered that all popular places, all sites, actually used by the people, tend to retain the best routine of antiquity very much more than any localities or machines used by any privileged class. Things are not altered so quickly or completely by common people as they are by fashionable people. Ruskin could have found more memories of the Middle Ages in the Underground Railway than in the grand hotels outside the stations. The great palaces of pleasure which the rich build in London all have brazen and vulgar names. Their names are either snobbish, like the Hotel Cecil, or (worse still) cosmopolitan like the Hotel Metropole. But when I go in a third-class carriage from the nearest circle station to Battersea to the nearest circle station to the Daily News, the names of the stations are one long litany of solemn and saintly memories. Leaving Victoria I come to a park belonging especially to St. James the Apostle; thence I go to Westminster Bridge, whose very name alludes to the awful Abbey; Charing Cross holds up the symbol of

Christendom; the next station is called a Temple; and Blackfriars remembers the mediaeval dream of a Brotherhood.

If you wish to find the past preserved, follow the million feet of the crowd. At the worst the uneducated only wear down old things by sheer walking. But the educated kick them down out of sheer culture.

I feel all this profoundly as I wander about the empty railway station, where I have no business of any kind. I have extracted a vast number of chocolates from automatic machines; I have obtained cigarettes, toffee, scent, and other things that I dislike by the same machinery; I have weighed myself, with sublime results; and this sense, not only of the healthiness of popular things, but of their essential antiquity and permanence, is still in possession of my mind. I wander up to the bookstall, and my faith survives even the wild spectacle of modern literature and journalism. Even in the crudest and most clamorous aspects of the newspaper world I still prefer the popular to the proud and fastidious. If I had to choose between taking in the DAILY MAIL and taking in the TIMES (the dilemma reminds one of a nightmare), I should certainly cry out with the whole of my being for the DAILY MAIL. Even mere bigness preached in a frivolous way is not so irritating as mere meanness preached in a big and solemn way. People buy the DAILY MAIL, but they do not believe in it. They do believe in the TIMES, and (apparently) they do not buy it. But the more the output of paper upon the modern world is actually studied, the more it will be found to be in all its essentials ancient and human, like the name of Charing Cross. Linger for two or three hours at a station bookstall (as I am doing), and you will find that it gradually takes on the grandeur and historic allusiveness of the Vatican or Bodleian Library. The novelty is all superficial; the tradition is all interior and profound. The DAILY MAIL has new editions, but never a new idea. Everything in a newspaper that is not the old human love of altar or fatherland is the old human love of gossip. Modern writers have often made game of the old chronicles because they chiefly record accidents and prodigies; a church struck by lightning, or a calf with six legs. They do not seem to realise that this old barbaric history is the same as new democratic journalism. It is not that the savage chronicle has disappeared. It is merely that the savage chronicle now appears every morning.

As I moved thus mildly and vaguely in front of the bookstall, my eye caught a sudden and scarlet title that for the moment staggered me. On the outside of a book I saw written in large letters, "Get On or Get Out."

The title of the book recalled to me with a sudden revolt and reaction all that does seem unquestionably new and nasty; it reminded me that there was in the world of to-day that utterly idiotic thing, a worship of success; a thing that only means surpassing anybody in anything; a thing that may mean being the most successful person in running away from a battle; a thing that may mean being the most successfully sleepy of the whole row of sleeping men. When I saw those words the silence and sanctity of the railway station were for the moment shadowed. Here, I thought, there is at any rate something anarchic and violent and vile. This title, at any rate, means the most disgusting individualism of this individualistic world. In the fury of my bitterness and passion I actually bought the book, thereby ensuring that my enemy would get some of my money. I opened it prepared to find some brutality, some blasphemy, which would really be an exception to the general silence and sanctity of the railway station. I was prepared to find something in the book that was as infamous as its title.

I was disappointed. There was nothing at all corresponding to the furious decisiveness of the remarks on the cover. After reading it carefully I could not discover whether I was really to get on or to get out; but I had a vague feeling that I should prefer to get out. A considerable part of the book, particularly towards the end, was concerned with a detailed description of the life of Napoleon Bonaparte. Undoubtedly Napoleon got on. He also got out. But I could not discover in any way how the details of his life given here were supposed to help a person aiming at success. One anecdote described how Napoleon always wiped his pen on his knee-breeches. I suppose the moral is: always wipe your pen on your knee-breeches, and you will win the battle of Wagram. Another story told that he let loose a gazelle among the ladies of his Court. Clearly the brutal practical inference is—loose a gazelle among the ladies of your acquaintance, and you will be Emperor of the French. Get on with a gazelle or get out. The book entirely reconciled me to the soft twilight of the station. Then I suddenly saw that there was a symbolic division which might be paralleled from biology. Brave men are vertebrates; they have their softness on the surface and their toughness in the middle. But these modern cowards are all crustaceans; their hardness is all on the cover and their softness is inside. But the softness is there; everything in this twilight temple is soft.

XXXIV

The Diabolist

Every now and then I have introduced into my essays an element of truth. Things that really happened have been mentioned, such as meeting President Kruger or being thrown out of a cab. What I have now to relate really happened; yet there was no element in it of practical politics or of personal danger. It was simply a quiet conversation which I had with another man. But that quiet conversation was by far the most terrible thing that has ever happened to me in my life. It happened so long ago that I cannot be certain of the exact words of the dialogue, only of its main questions and answers; but there is one sentence in it for which I can answer absolutely and word for word. It was a sentence so awful that I could not forget it if I would. It was the last sentence spoken; and it was not spoken to me.

The thing befell me in the days when I was at an art school. An art school is different from almost all other schools or colleges in this respect: that, being of new and crude creation and of lax discipline, it presents a specially strong contrast between the industrious and the idle. People at an art school either do an atrocious amount of work or do no work at all. I belonged, along with other charming people, to the latter class; and this threw me often into the society of men who were very different from myself, and who were idle for reasons very different from mine. I was idle because I was very much occupied; I was engaged about that time in discovering, to my own extreme and lasting astonishment, that I was not an atheist. But there were others also at loose ends who were engaged in discovering what Carlyle called (I think with needless delicacy) the fact that ginger is hot in the mouth.

I value that time, in short, because it made me acquainted with a good representative number of blackguards. In this connection there are two very curious things which the critic of human life may observe. The first is the fact that there is one real difference between men and women; that women prefer to talk in twos, while men prefer to talk in threes. The second is that when you find (as you often do) three young cads and idiots going about together and getting drunk together every day you generally find that one of the three cads and idiots is (for some extraordinary reason) not a cad and not an idiot. In these small groups devoted to a drivelling dissipation there is almost always one man who seems to have condescended to his company; one man who, while he can talk a foul triviality with his fellows, can also talk politics with a Socialist, or philosophy with a Catholic.

It was just such a man whom I came to know well. It was strange, perhaps, that he liked his dirty, drunken society; it was stranger still, perhaps, that he liked my society. For hours of the day he would talk with me about Milton or Gothic architecture; for hours of the night he would go where I have no wish to follow him, even in speculation. He was a man with a long, ironical face, and close and red hair; he was by class a gentleman, and could walk like one, but preferred, for some reason, to walk like a groom carrying two pails. He looked like a sort of Super-jockey; as if some archangel had gone on the Turf. And I shall never forget the half-hour in which he and I argued about real things for the first and the last time.

ALONG THE FRONT OF THE big building of which our school was a part ran a huge slope of stone steps, higher, I think, than those that lead up to St. Paul's Cathedral. On a black wintry evening he and I were wandering on these cold heights, which seemed as dreary as a pyramid under the stars. The one thing visible below us in the blackness was a burning and blowing fire; for some gardener (I suppose) was burning something in the grounds, and from time to time the red sparks went whirling past us like a swarm of scarlet insects in the dark. Above us also it was gloom; but if one stared long enough at that upper darkness, one saw vertical stripes of grey in the black and then became conscious of the colossal façade of the Doric building, phantasmal, yet filling the sky, as if Heaven were still filled with the gigantic ghost of Paganism.

THE MAN ASKED ME ABRUPTLY why I was becoming orthodox. Until he said it, I really had not known that I was; but the moment he had said it I knew it to be literally true. And the process had been so long and full that I answered him at once out of existing stores of explanation.

"I am becoming orthodox," I said, "because I have come, rightly or wrongly, after stretching my brain till it bursts, to the old belief that heresy is worse even than sin. An error is more menacing than a crime, for an error begets crimes. An Imperialist is worse than a pirate. For an Imperialist keeps a school for pirates; he teaches piracy disinterestedly and without an adequate salary. A Free Lover is worse than a profligate.

For a profligate is serious and reckless even in his shortest love; while a Free Lover is cautious and irresponsible even in his longest devotion. I hate modern doubt because it is dangerous."

"You mean dangerous to morality," he said in a voice of wonderful gentleness. "I expect you are right. But why do you care about morality?"

I glanced at his face quickly. He had thrust out his neck as he had a trick of doing; and so brought his face abruptly into the light of the bonfire from below, like a face in the footlights. His long chin and high cheek-bones were lit up infernally from underneath; so that he looked like a fiend staring down into the flaming pit. I had an unmeaning sense of being tempted in a wilderness; and even as I paused a burst of red sparks broke past.

"Aren't those sparks splendid?" I said.

"Yes," he replied.

"That is all that I ask you to admit," said I. "Give me those few red specks and I will deduce Christian morality. Once I thought like you, that one's pleasure in a flying spark was a thing that could come and go with that spark. Once I thought that the delight was as free as the fire. Once I thought that red star we see was alone in space. But now I know that the red star is only on the apex of an invisible pyramid of virtues. That red fire is only the flower on a stalk of living habits, which you cannot see. Only because your mother made you say 'Thank you' for a bun are you now able to thank Nature or chaos for those red stars of an instant or for the white stars of all time. Only because you were humble before fireworks on the fifth of November do you now enjoy any fireworks that you chance to see. You only like them being red because you were told about the blood of the martyrs; you only like them being bright because brightness is a glory. That flame flowered out of virtues, and it will fade with virtues. Seduce a woman, and that spark will be less bright. Shed blood, and that spark will be less red. Be really bad, and they will be to you like the spots on a wall-paper."

He had a horrible fairness of the intellect that made me despair of his soul. A common, harmless atheist would have denied that religion produced humility or humility a simple joy: but he admitted both. He only said, "But shall I not find in evil a life of its own? Granted that for every woman I ruin one of those red sparks will go out: will not the expanding pleasure of ruin. . ."

"Do you see that fire?" I asked. "If we had a real fighting democracy, some one would burn you in it; like the devil-worshipper that you are."

"Perhaps," he said, in his tired, fair way. "Only what you call evil I call good."

He went down the great steps alone, and I felt as if I wanted the steps swept and cleaned. I followed later, and as I went to find my hat in the low, dark passage where it hung, I suddenly heard his voice again, but the words were inaudible. I stopped, startled: then I heard the voice of one of the vilest of his associates saying, "Nobody can possibly know." And then I heard those two or three words which I remember in every syllable and cannot forget. I heard the Diabolist say, "I tell you I have done everything else. If I do that I shan't know the difference between right and wrong." I rushed out without daring to pause; and as I passed the fire I did not know whether it was hell or the furious love of God.

I have since heard that he died: it may be said, I think, that he committed suicide; though he did it with tools of pleasure, not with tools of pain. God help him, I know the road he went; but I have never known, or even dared to think, what was that place at which he stopped and refrained.

XXXV

A Glimpse of My Country

Whatever is it that we are all looking for? I fancy that it is really quite close. When I was a boy I had a fancy that Heaven or Fairyland or whatever I called it, was immediately behind my own back, and that this was why I could never manage to see it, however often I twisted and turned to take it by surprise. I had a notion of a man perpetually spinning round on one foot like a teetotum in the effort to find that world behind his back which continually fled from him. Perhaps this is why the world goes round. Perhaps the world is always trying to look over its shoulder and catch up the world which always escapes it, yet without which it cannot be itself.

In any case, as I have said, I think that we must always conceive of that which is the goal of all our endeavours as something which is in some strange way near. Science boasts of the distance of its stars; of the terrific remoteness of the things of which it has to speak. But poetry and religion always insist upon the proximity, the almost menacing closeness of the things with which they are concerned. Always the Kingdom of Heaven is "At Hand"; and Looking-glass Land is only through the looking-glass. So I for one should never be astonished if the next twist of a street led me to the heart of that maze in which all the mystics are lost. I should not be at all surprised if I turned one corner in Fleet Street and saw a yet queerer-looking lamp; I should not be surprised if I turned a third corner and found myself in Elfland.

I should not be surprised at this; but I was surprised the other day at something more surprising. I took a turn out of Fleet Street and found myself in England.

The singular shock experienced perhaps requires explanation. In the darkest or the most inadequate moments of England there is one thing that should always be remembered about the very nature of our country. It may be shortly stated by saying that England is not such a fool as it looks. The types of England, the externals of England, always misrepresent the country. England is an oligarchical country, and it prefers that its oligarchy should be inferior to itself.

The speaking in the House of Commons, for instance, is not only worse than the speaking was, it is worse than the speaking is, in all or almost all other places in small debating clubs or casual dinners. Our countrymen probably prefer this solemn futility in the higher places of the national life. It may be a strange sight to see the blind leading the blind; but England provides a stranger. England shows us the blind leading the people who can see. And this again is an under-statement of the case. For the English political aristocrats not only speak worse than many other people; they speak worse than themselves. The ignorance of statesmen is like the ignorance of judges, an artificial and affected thing. If you have the good fortune really to talk with a statesman, you will be constantly startled with his saying quite intelligent things. It makes one nervous at first. And I have never been sufficiently intimate with such a man to ask him why it was a rule of his life in Parliament to appear sillier than he was.

It is the same with the voters. The average man votes below himself; he votes with half a mind or with a hundredth part of one. A man ought to vote with the whole of himself as he worships or gets married. A man ought to vote with his head and heart, his soul and stomach, his eye for faces and his ear for music; also (when sufficiently provoked) with his hands and feet. If he has ever seen a fine sunset, the crimson colour of it should creep into his vote. If he has ever heard splendid songs, they should be in his ears when he makes the mystical cross. But as it is, the difficulty with English democracy at all elections is that it is something less than itself. The question is not so much whether only a minority of the electorate votes. The point is that only a minority of the voter votes.

THIS IS THE TRAGEDY OF England; you cannot judge it by its foremost men. Its types do not typify. And on the occasion of which I speak I found this to be so especially of that old intelligent middle class which I had imagined had almost vanished from the world. It seemed to me that all the main representatives of the middle class had gone off in one direction or in the other; they had either set out in pursuit of the Smart Set or they had set out in pursuit of the Simple Life. I cannot say which I dislike more myself; the people in question are welcome to have either of them, or, as is more likely, to have both, in hideous alternations of disease and cure. But all the prominent men who plainly represent the middle class have adopted either the single eye-glass of Mr. Chamberlain or the single eye of Mr. Bernard Shaw.

The old class that I mean has no representative. Its food was plentiful; but it had no show. Its food was plain; but it had no fads. It was serious about politics; and when it spoke in public it committed the solecism of trying to speak well. I thought that this old earnest political England had practically disappeared. And as I say, I took one turn out of Fleet Street and I found a room full of it.

AT THE TOP OF THE room was a chair in which Johnson had sat. The club was a club in which Wilkes had spoken, in a time when even the ne'er-do-weel was virile. But all these things by themselves might be merely archaism. The extraordinary thing was that this hall had all the hubbub, the sincerity, the anger, the oratory of the eighteenth century. The members of this club were of all shades of opinion, yet there was not one speech which gave me that jar of unreality which I often have in listening to the ablest men uttering my own opinion. The Toryism of this club was like the Toryism of Johnson, a Toryism that could use humour and appealed to humanity. The democracy of this club was like the democracy of Wilkes, a democracy that can speak epigrams and fight duels; a democracy that can face things out and endure slander; the democracy of Wilkes, or, rather, the democracy of Fox.

One thing especially filled my soul with the soul of my fathers. Each man speaking, whether he spoke well or ill, spoke as well as he could from sheer fury against the other man. This is the greatest of our modern descents, that nowadays a man does not become more rhetorical as he becomes more sincere. An eighteenth-century speaker, when he got really and honestly furious, looked for big words with which to crush his adversary. The new speaker looks for small words to crush him with. He looks for little facts and little sneers. In a modern speech the rhetoric is put into the merely formal part, the opening to which nobody listens. But when Mr. Chamberlain, or a Moderate, or one of the harder kind of Socialists, becomes really sincere, he becomes Cockney. "The destiny of the Empire," or "The destiny of humanity," do well enough for mere ornamental preliminaries, but when the man becomes angry and honest, then it is a snarl, "Where do we come in?" or "It's your money they want."

The men in this eighteenth-century club were entirely different; they were quite eighteenth century. Each one rose to his feet quivering with passion, and tried to destroy his opponent, not with sniggering, but actually with eloquence. I was arguing with them about Home Rule; at the end I told them why the English aristocracy really disliked an Irish Parliament; because it would be like their club.

I CAME OUT AGAIN INTO Fleet Street at night, and by a dim lamp I saw pasted up some tawdry nonsense about Wastrels and how London was rising against something that London had hardly heard of. Then I suddenly saw, as in one obvious picture, that the modern world is an immense and tumultuous ocean, full of monstrous and living things. And I saw that across the top of it is spread a thin, a very thin, sheet of ice, of wicked wealth and of lying journalism.

And as I stood there in the darkness I could almost fancy that I heard it crack.

XXXVI

A Somewhat Improbable Story

I cannot remember whether this tale is true or not. If I read it through very carefully I have a suspicion that I should come to the conclusion that it is not. But, unfortunately, I cannot read it through very carefully, because, you see, it is not written yet. The image and the idea of it clung to me through a great part of my boyhood; I may have dreamt it before I could talk; or told it to myself before I could read; or read it before I could remember. On the whole, however, I am certain that I did not read it, for children have very clear memories about things like that; and of the books which I was really fond I can still remember, not only the shape and bulk and binding, but even the position of the printed words on many of the pages. On the whole, I incline to the opinion that it happened to me before I was born.

At any rate, let us tell the story now with all the advantages of the atmosphere that has clung to it. You may suppose me, for the sake of argument, sitting at lunch in one of those quick-lunch restaurants in the City where men take their food so fast that it has none of the quality of food, and take their half-hour's vacation so fast that it has none of the qualities of leisure; to hurry through one's leisure is the most unbusiness-like of actions. They all wore tall shiny hats as if they could not lose an instant even to hang them on a peg, and they all had one eye a little off, hypnotised by the huge eye of the clock. In short, they were the slaves of the modern bondage, you could hear their fetters clanking. Each was, in fact, bound by a chain; the heaviest chain ever tied to a man—it is called a watch-chain.

Now, among these there entered and sat down opposite to me a man who almost immediately opened an uninterrupted monologue. He was like all the other men in dress, yet he was startlingly opposite to them in all manner. He wore a high shiny hat and a long frock coat, but he wore them as such solemn things were meant to be worn; he wore the silk hat as if it were a mitre, and the frock coat as if it were the ephod of a high priest. He not only hung his hat up on the peg, but he seemed (such was his stateliness) almost to ask permission of the hat for doing so, and to apologise to the peg for making use of it. When he had sat down on a wooden chair with the air of one considering its feelings and given a sort of slight stoop or bow to the wooden table itself, as if it were an altar, I could not help some comment springing to my lips. For the man was a big, sanguine-faced, prosperous-looking man, and yet he treated everything with a care that almost amounted to nervousness.

For the sake of saying something to express my interest I said, "This furniture is fairly solid; but, of course, people do treat it much too carelessly."

As I looked up doubtfully my eye caught his, and was fixed as his was fixed in an apocalyptic stare. I had thought him ordinary as he entered, save for his strange, cautious manner; but if the other people had seen him then they would have screamed and emptied the room. They did not see him, and they went on making a clatter with their forks, and a murmur with their conversation. But the man's face was the face of a maniac.

"Did you mean anything particular by that remark?" he asked at last, and the blood crawled back slowly into his face.

"Nothing whatever," I answered. "One does not mean anything here; it spoils people's digestions."

He limped back and wiped his broad forehead with a big handkerchief; and yet there seemed to be a sort of regret in his relief.

"I thought perhaps," he said in a low voice, "that another of them had gone wrong."

"If you mean another digestion gone wrong," I said, "I never heard of one here that went right. This is the heart of the Empire, and the other organs are in an equally bad way."

"No, I mean another street gone wrong," and he said heavily and quietly, "but as I suppose that doesn't explain much to you, I think I shall have to tell you the story. I do so with all the less responsibility, because I know you won't believe it. For forty years of my life I invariably left my office, which is in Leadenhall Street, at half-past five in the afternoon, taking with me an umbrella in the right hand and a bag in the left hand. For forty years two months and four days I passed out of the side office door, walked down the street on the left-hand side, took the first turning to the left and the third to the right, from where I bought an evening paper, followed the road on the right-hand side round two obtuse angles, and came out just outside a Metropolitan station, where I took a train home. For forty years two months and four days I fulfilled this course by accumulated habit: it was not a long street that I traversed, and it took me about four and a half minutes to do it. After forty years two months and four days, on the fifth day I went out in the same manner, with my umbrella in the right hand and my bag in the left, and I began to notice that walking along the familiar street tired me somewhat more than usual; and when I turned it I was convinced that I had turned down the wrong one. For now the street shot up quite a steep slant, such as one only sees in the hilly parts of London, and in this part there were no hills at all. Yet it was not the wrong street; the name written on it was the same; the shuttered shops were the same; the lamp-posts and the whole look of the perspective was the same; only it was tilted upwards like a lid. Forgetting any trouble about breathlessness or fatigue I ran furiously forward, and reached the second of my accustomed turnings, which ought to bring me almost within sight of the station. And as I turned that corner I nearly fell on the pavement. For now the street went up straight in front of my face like a steep staircase or the side of a pyramid. There was not for miles round that place so much as a slope like that of Ludgate Hill. And this was a slope like that of the Matterhorn. The whole street had lifted itself like a single wave, and yet every speck and detail of it was the same, and I saw in the high distance, as at the top of an Alpine pass, picked out in pink letters the name over my paper shop.

"I ran on and on blindly now, passing all the shops and coming to a part of the road where there was a long grey row of private houses. I had, I know not why, an irrational feeling that I was a long iron bridge in empty space. An impulse seized me, and I pulled up the iron trap of a coal-hole. Looking down through it I saw empty space and the stars.

"When I looked up again a man was standing in his front garden, having apparently come out of his house; he was leaning over the railings and gazing at me. We were all alone on that nightmare road; his face was in shadow; his dress was dark and ordinary; but when I saw him standing so perfectly still I knew somehow that he was not of this world. And the stars behind his head were larger and fiercer than ought to be endured by the eyes of men.

"'If you are a kind angel,' I said, 'or a wise devil, or have anything in common with mankind, tell me what is this street possessed of devils.'

"After a long silence he said, 'What do you say that it is?'

"'It is Bumpton Street, of course,' I snapped. 'It goes to Oldgate Station.'

"'Yes,' he admitted gravely; 'it goes there sometimes. Just now, however, it is going to heaven.'

"'To heaven?' I said. 'Why?'

"'It is going to heaven for justice,' he replied. 'You must have treated it badly. Remember always that there is one thing that cannot be endured by anybody or anything. That one unendurable thing is to be overworked and also neglected. For instance, you can overwork women—everybody does. But you can't neglect women—I defy you to. At the same time, you can neglect tramps and gypsies and all the apparent refuse of the State so long as you do not overwork it. But no beast of the field, no horse, no dog can endure long to be asked to do more than his work and yet have less than his honour. It is the same with streets. You have worked this street to death, and yet you have never remembered its existence. If you had a healthy democracy, even of pagans, they would have hung this street with garlands and given it the name of a god. Then it would have gone quietly. But at last the street has grown tired of your tireless insolence; and it is bucking and rearing its head to heaven. Have you never sat on a bucking horse?'

"I looked at the long grey street, and for a moment it seemed to me to be exactly like the long grey neck of a horse flung up to heaven. But in a moment my sanity returned, and I said, 'But this is all nonsense. Streets go to the place they have to go. A street must always go to its end.'

"'Why do you think so of a street?' he asked, standing very still.

"'Because I have always seen it do the same thing,' I replied, in reasonable anger. 'Day after day, year after year, it has always gone to Oldgate Station; day after. . .'

"I stopped, for he had flung up his head with the fury of the road in revolt.

"'And you?' he cried terribly. 'What do you think the road thinks of you? Does the road think you are alive? Are you alive? Day after day, year after year, you have gone to Oldgate Station. . .' Since then I have respected the things called inanimate."

And bowing slightly to the mustard-pot, the man in the restaurant withdrew.

XXXVII

The Shop of Ghosts

Nearly all the best and most precious things in the universe you can get for a halfpenny. I make an exception, of course, of the sun, the moon, the earth, people, stars, thunderstorms, and such trifles. You can get them for nothing. Also I make an exception of another thing, which I am not allowed to mention in this paper, and of which the lowest price is a penny halfpenny. But the general principle will be at once apparent. In the street behind me, for instance, you can now get a ride on an electric tram for a halfpenny. To be on an electric tram is to be on a flying castle in a fairy tale. You can get quite a large number of brightly coloured sweets for a halfpenny. Also you can get the chance of reading this article for a halfpenny; along, of course, with other and irrelevant matter.

But if you want to see what a vast and bewildering array of valuable things you can get at a halfpenny each you should do as I was doing last night. I was gluing my nose against the glass of a very small and dimly lit toy shop in one of the greyest and leanest of the streets of Battersea. But dim as was that square of light, it was filled (as a child once said to me) with all the colours God ever made. Those toys of the poor were like the children who buy them; they were all dirty; but they were all bright. For my part, I think brightness more important than cleanliness; since the first is of the soul, and the second of the body. You must excuse me; I am a democrat; I know I am out of fashion in the modern world.

As I looked at that palace of pigmy wonders, at small green omnibuses, at small blue elephants, at small black dolls, and small red Noah's arks, I must have fallen into some sort of unnatural trance. That lit shop-window became like the brilliantly lit stage when one is watching some highly coloured comedy. I forgot the grey houses and the grimy people behind me as one forgets the dark galleries and the dim crowds at a theatre. It seemed as if the little objects behind the glass were small, not because they were toys, but because they were objects far away. The green omnibus was really a green omnibus, a green

Bayswater omnibus, passing across some huge desert on its ordinary way to Bayswater. The blue elephant was no longer blue with paint; he was blue with distance. The black doll was really a negro relieved against passionate tropic foliage in the land where every weed is flaming and only man is black. The red Noah's ark was really the enormous ship of earthly salvation riding on the rain-swollen sea, red in the first morning of hope.

Every one, I suppose, knows such stunning instants of abstraction, such brilliant blanks in the mind. In such moments one can see the face of one's own best friend as an unmeaning pattern of spectacles or moustaches. They are commonly marked by the two signs of the slowness of their growth and the suddenness of their termination. The return to real thinking is often as abrupt as bumping into a man. Very often indeed (in my case) it is bumping into a man. But in any case the awakening is always emphatic and, generally speaking, it is always complete. Now, in this case, I did come back with a shock of sanity to the consciousness that I was, after all, only staring into a dingy little toy-shop; but in some strange way the mental cure did not seem to be final. There was still in my mind an unmanageable something that told me that I had strayed into some odd atmosphere, or that I had already done some odd thing. I felt as if I had worked a miracle or committed a sin. It was as if I had at any rate, stepped across some border in the soul.

To shake off this dangerous and dreamy sense I went into the shop and tried to buy wooden soldiers. The man in the shop was very old and broken, with confused white hair covering his head and half his face, hair so startlingly white that it looked almost artificial. Yet though he was senile and even sick, there was nothing of suffering in his eyes; he looked rather as if he were gradually falling asleep in a not unkindly decay. He gave me the wooden soldiers, but when I put down the money he did not at first seem to see it; then he blinked at it feebly, and then he pushed it feebly away.

"No, no," he said vaguely. "I never have. I never have. We are rather old-fashioned here."

"Not taking money," I replied, "seems to me more like an uncommonly new fashion than an old one."

"I never have," said the old man, blinking and blowing his nose; "I've always given presents. I'm too old to stop."

"Good heavens!" I said. "What can you mean? Why, you might be Father Christmas."

"I am Father Christmas," he said apologetically, and blew his nose again.

The lamps could not have been lighted yet in the street outside. At any rate, I could see nothing against the darkness but the shining shop-window. There were no sounds of steps or voices in the street; I might have strayed into some new and sunless world. But something had cut the chords of common sense, and I could not feel even surprise except sleepily. Something made me say, "You look ill, Father Christmas."

"I am dying," he said.

I did not speak, and it was he who spoke again.

"All the new people have left my shop. I cannot understand it. They seem to object to me on such curious and inconsistent sort of grounds, these scientific men, and these innovators. They say that I give people superstitions and make them too visionary; they say I give people sausages and make them too coarse. They say my heavenly parts are too heavenly; they say my earthly parts are too earthly; I don't know what they want, I'm sure. How can heavenly things be too heavenly, or earthly things too earthly? How can one be too good, or too jolly? I don't understand. But I understand one thing well enough. These modern people are living and I am dead."

"You may be dead," I replied. "You ought to know. But as for what they are doing, do not call it living."

A SILENCE FELL SUDDENLY BETWEEN us which I somehow expected to be unbroken. But it had not fallen for more than a few seconds when, in the utter stillness, I distinctly heard a very rapid step coming nearer and nearer along the street. The next moment a figure flung itself into the shop and stood framed in the doorway. He wore a large white hat tilted back as if in impatience; he had tight black old-fashioned pantaloons, a gaudy old-fashioned stock and waistcoat, and an old fantastic coat. He had large, wide-open, luminous eyes like those of an arresting actor; he had a pale, nervous face, and a fringe of beard. He took in the shop and the old man in a look that seemed literally a flash and uttered the exclamation of a man utterly staggered.

"Good lord!" he cried out; "it can't be you! It isn't you! I came to ask where your grave was."

"I'm not dead yet, Mr. Dickens," said the old gentleman, with a feeble smile; "but I'm dying," he hastened to add reassuringly.

"But, dash it all, you were dying in my time," said Mr. Charles Dickens with animation; "and you don't look a day older."

"I've felt like this for a long time," said Father Christmas.

Mr. Dickens turned his back and put his head out of the door into the darkness.

"Dick," he roared at the top of his voice; "he's still alive."

ANOTHER SHADOW DARKENED THE DOORWAY, and a much larger and more full-blooded gentleman in an enormous periwig came in, fanning his flushed face with a military hat of the cut of Queen Anne. He carried his head well back like a soldier, and his hot face had even a look of arrogance, which was suddenly contradicted by his eyes, which were literally as humble as a dog's. His sword made a great clatter, as if the shop were too small for it.

"Indeed," said Sir Richard Steele, "'tis a most prodigious matter, for the man was dying when I wrote about Sir Roger de Coverley and his Christmas Day."

My senses were growing dimmer and the room darker. It seemed to be filled with newcomers.

"It hath ever been understood," said a burly man, who carried his head humorously and obstinately a little on one side—I think he was Ben Jonson—"It hath ever been understood, consule Jacobo, under our King James and her late Majesty, that such good and hearty customs were fallen sick, and like to pass from the world. This grey beard most surely was no lustier when I knew him than now."

And I also thought I heard a green-clad man, like Robin Hood, say in some mixed Norman French, "But I saw the man dying."

"I have felt like this a long time," said Father Christmas, in his feeble way again.

Mr. Charles Dickens suddenly leant across to him.

"Since when?" he asked. "Since you were born?"

"Yes," said the old man, and sank shaking into a chair. "I have been always dying."

Mr. Dickens took off his hat with a flourish like a man calling a mob to rise.

"I understand it now," he cried, "you will never die."

XXXVIII

The Ballade of a Strange Town

My friend and I, in fooling about Flanders, fell into a fixed affection for the town of Mechlin or Malines. Our rest there was so restful that we almost felt it as a home, and hardly strayed out of it.

We sat day after day in the market-place, under little trees growing in wooden tubs, and looked up at the noble converging lines of the Cathedral tower, from which the three riders from Ghent, in the poem, heard the bell which told them they were not too late. But we took as much pleasure in the people, in the little boys with open, flat Flemish faces and fur collars round their necks, making them look like burgomasters; or the women, whose prim, oval faces, hair strained tightly off the temples, and mouths at once hard, meek, and humorous, exactly reproduced the late mediaeval faces in Memling and Van Eyck.

But one afternoon, as it happened, my friend rose from under his little tree, and pointing to a sort of toy train that was puffing smoke in one corner of the clear square, suggested that we should go by it. We got into the little train, which was meant really to take the peasants and their vegetables to and fro from their fields beyond the town, and the official came round to give us tickets. We asked him what place we should get to if we paid fivepence. The Belgians are not a romantic people, and he asked us (with a lamentable mixture of Flemish coarseness and French rationalism) where we wanted to go.

We explained that we wanted to go to fairyland, and the only question was whether we could get there for fivepence. At last, after a great deal of international misunderstanding (for he spoke French in the Flemish and we in the English manner), he told us that fivepence would take us to a place which I have never seen written down, but which when spoken sounded like the word "Waterloo" pronounced by an intoxicated patriot; I think it was Waerlowe.

We clasped our hands and said it was the place we had been seeking from boyhood, and when we had got there we descended with promptitude.

For a moment I had a horrible fear that it really was the field of Waterloo; but I was comforted by remembering that it was in quite a different part of Belgium. It was a cross-roads, with one cottage at the corner, a perspective of tall trees like Hobbema's "Avenue," and beyond only the infinite flat chess-board of the little fields. It was the scene of peace and prosperity; but I must confess that my friend's first action was to ask the man when there would be another train back to Mechlin. The man stated that there would be a train back in exactly one hour. We walked up the avenue, and when we were nearly half an hour's walk away it began to rain.

WE ARRIVED BACK AT THE cross-roads sodden and dripping, and, finding the train waiting, climbed into it with some relief. The officer on this train could speak nothing but Flemish, but he understood the name Mechlin, and indicated that when we came to Mechlin Station he would put us down, which, after the right interval of time, he did.

We got down, under a steady downpour, evidently on the edge of Mechlin, though the features could not easily be recognised through the grey screen of the rain. I do not generally agree with those who find rain depressing. A shower-bath is not depressing; it is rather startling. And if it is exciting when a man throws a pail of water over you, why should it not also be exciting when the gods throw many pails? But on this soaking afternoon, whether it was the dull sky-line of the Netherlands or the fact that we were returning home without any adventure, I really did think things a trifle dreary. As soon as we could creep under the shelter of a street we turned into a little café, kept by one woman. She was incredibly old, and she spoke no French. There we drank black coffee and what was called "cognac fine." "Cognac fine" were the only two French words used in the establishment, and they were not true. At least, the fineness (perhaps by its very ethereal delicacy) escaped me. After a little my friend, who was more restless than I, got up and went out, to see if the rain had stopped and if we could at once stroll back to our hotel by the station. I sat finishing my coffee in a colourless mood, and listening to the unremitting rain.

SUDDENLY THE DOOR BURST OPEN, and my friend appeared, transfigured and frantic.

"Get up!" he cried, waving his hands wildly. "Get up! We're in the wrong town! We're not in Mechlin at all. Mechlin is ten miles, twenty miles off—God knows what! We're somewhere near Antwerp."

"What!" I cried, leaping from my seat, and sending the furniture flying. "Then all is well, after all! Poetry only hid her face for an instant behind a cloud. Positively for a moment I was feeling depressed because we were in the right town. But if we are in the wrong town—why, we have our adventure after all! If we are in the wrong town, we are in the right place."

I rushed out into the rain, and my friend followed me somewhat more grimly. We discovered we were in a town called Lierre, which seemed to consist chiefly of bankrupt pastry cooks, who sold lemonade.

"This is the peak of our whole poetic progress!" I cried enthusiastically. "We must do something, something sacramental and commemorative! We cannot sacrifice an ox, and it would be a bore to build a temple. Let us write a poem."

With but slight encouragement, I took out an old envelope and one of those pencils that turn bright violet in water. There was plenty of water about, and the violet ran down the paper, symbolising the rich purple of that romantic hour. I began, choosing the form of an old French ballade; it is the easiest because it is the most restricted—

> *"Can Man to Mount Olympus rise,*
> *And fancy Primrose Hill the scene?*
> *Can a man walk in Paradise*
> *And think he is in Turnham Green?*
> *And could I take you for Malines,*
> *Not knowing the nobler thing you were?*
> *O Pearl of all the plain, and queen,*
> *The lovely city of Lierre.*

> *"Through memory's mist in glimmering guise*
> *Shall shine your streets of sloppy sheen.*
> *And wet shall grow my dreaming eyes,*
> *To think how wet my boots have been*
> *Now if I die or shoot a Dean—"*

Here I broke off to ask my friend whether he thought it expressed a more wild calamity to shoot a Dean or to be a Dean. But he only turned up his coat collar, and I felt that for him the muse had folded her wings. I rewrote—

> *"Now if I die a Rural Dean,*
> *Or rob a bank I do not care,*
> *Or turn a Tory. I have seen*
> *The lovely city of Lierre."*

"The next line," I resumed, warming to it; but my friend interrupted me.

"The next line," he said somewhat harshly, "will be a railway line. We can get back to Mechlin from here, I find, though we have to change twice. I dare say I should think this jolly romantic but for the weather. Adventure is the champagne of life, but I prefer my champagne and my adventures dry. Here is the station."

WE DID NOT SPEAK AGAIN until we had left Lierre, in its sacred cloud of rain, and were coming to Mechlin, under a clearer sky, that even made one think of stars. Then I leant forward and said to my friend in a low voice—"I have found out everything. We have come to the wrong star."

He stared his query, and I went on eagerly: "That is what makes life at once so splendid and so strange. We are in the wrong world. When I thought that was the right town, it bored me; when I knew it was wrong, I was happy. So the false optimism, the modern happiness, tires us because it tells us we fit into this world. The true happiness is that we don't fit. We come from somewhere else. We have lost our way."

He silently nodded, staring out of the window, but whether I had impressed or only fatigued him I could not tell. "This," I added, "is suggested in the last verse of a fine poem you have grossly neglected—

> *"Happy is he and more than wise*
> *Who sees with wondering eyes and clean*
> *The world through all the grey disguise*
> *Of sleep and custom in between.*
> *Yes; we may pass the heavenly screen,*
> *But shall we know when we are there?*
> *Who know not what these dead stones mean,*
> *The lovely city of Lierre."*

Here the train stopped abruptly. And from Mechlin church steeple we heard the half-chime: and Joris broke silence with "No bally HORS D'OEUVRES for me: I shall get on to something solid at once."

L'Envoy

Prince, wide your Empire spreads, I ween,
Yet happier is that moistened Mayor,
Who drinks her cognac far from fine,
The lovely city of Lierre.

XXXIX

The Mystery of a Pageant

Once upon a time, it seems centuries ago, I was prevailed on to take a small part in one of those historical processions or pageants which happened to be fashionable in or about the year 1909. And since I tend, like all who are growing old, to re-enter the remote past as a paradise or playground, I disinter a memory which may serve to stand among those memories of small but strange incidents with which I have sometimes filled this column. The thing has really some of the dark qualities of a detective-story; though I suppose that Sherlock Holmes himself could hardly unravel it now, when the scent is so old and cold and most of the actors, doubtless, long dead.

This old pageant included a series of figures from the eighteenth century, and I was told that I was just like Dr. Johnson. Seeing that Dr. Johnson was heavily seamed with small-pox, had a waistcoat all over gravy, snorted and rolled as he walked, and was probably the ugliest man in London, I mention this identification as a fact and not as a vaunt. I had nothing to do with the arrangement; and such fleeting suggestions as I made were not taken so seriously as they might have been. I requested that a row of posts be erected across the lawn, so that I might touch all of them but one, and then go back and touch that. Failing this, I felt that the least they could do was to have twenty-five cups of tea stationed at regular intervals along the course, each held by a Mrs. Thrale in full costume. My best constructive suggestion was the most harshly rejected of all. In front of me in the procession walked the great Bishop Berkeley, the man who turned the tables on the early materialists by maintaining that matter itself possibly does not exist. Dr. Johnson, you will remember, did not like such bottomless fancies as Berkeley's, and kicked a stone with his foot, saying, "I refute him so!" Now (as I pointed out) kicking a stone would not make the metaphysical quarrel quite clear; besides, it would hurt. But how picturesque and perfect it would be if I moved across the ground in the symbolic attitude of kicking Bishop Berkeley! How complete an allegoric group; the great transcendentalist walking with his head among the stars, but behind him the avenging realist pede claudo, with uplifted foot. But I must not take up space with these forgotten frivolities; we old men grow too garrulous in talking of the distant past.

This story scarcely concerns me either in my real or my assumed character. Suffice it to say that the procession took place at night in a large garden and by torchlight (so remote is the date), that the garden was crowded with Puritans, monks, and men-at-arms, and especially with early Celtic saints smoking pipes, and with elegant Renaissance gentlemen talking Cockney. Suffice it to say, or rather it is needless to say, that I got lost. I wandered away into some dim corner of that dim shrubbery, where there was nothing to do except tumbling over tent ropes, and I began almost to feel like my prototype, and to share his horror of solitude and hatred of a country life.

In this detachment and dilemma I saw another man in a white wig advancing across this forsaken stretch of lawn; a tall, lean man, who stooped in his long black robes like a stooping eagle. When I thought he would pass me, he stopped before my face, and said, "Dr. Johnson, I think. I am Paley."

"Sir," I said, "you used to guide men to the beginnings of Christianity. If you can guide me now to wherever this infernal thing begins you will perform a yet higher and harder function."

His costume and style were so perfect that for the instant I really thought he was a ghost. He took no notice of my flippancy, but, turning his black-robed back on me, led me through verdurous glooms and winding mossy ways, until we came out into the glare of gaslight and laughing men in masquerade, and I could easily laugh at myself.

And there, you will say, was an end of the matter. I am (you will say) naturally obtuse, cowardly, and mentally deficient. I was, moreover, unused to pageants; I felt frightened in the dark and took a man for a spectre whom, in the light, I could recognise as a modern gentleman in a masquerade dress. No; far from it. That spectral person was my first introduction to a special incident which has never been explained and which still lays its finger on my nerve.

I mixed with the men of the eighteenth century; and we fooled as one does at a fancy-dress ball. There was Burke as large as life and a great deal better looking. There was Cowper much larger than life; he ought to have been a little man in a night-cap, with a cat under one arm and a spaniel under the other. As it was, he was a magnificent person, and looked more like the Master of Ballantrae than Cowper. I persuaded him at last to the night-cap, but never, alas, to the cat and dog. When I came the next night Burke was still the same beautiful improvement upon himself; Cowper was still weeping for his dog and cat and would not be comforted; Bishop Berkeley was still waiting to be kicked in the interests of philosophy. In short, I met all my old friends but one. Where was Paley? I had been mystically moved by the man's presence; I was moved more by his absence. At last I saw advancing towards us across the twilight garden a little man with a large book and a bright attractive face. When he came near enough he said, in a small, clear voice, "I'm Paley." The thing was quite natural, of course; the man was ill and had sent a substitute. Yet somehow the contrast was a shock.

By the next night I had grown quite friendly with my four or five colleagues; I had discovered what is called a mutual friend with Berkeley and several points of difference with Burke. Cowper, I think it was, who introduced me to a friend of his, a fresh face, square and sturdy, framed in a white wig. "This," he explained, "is my friend So-and-So. He's Paley." I looked round at all the faces by this time fixed and familiar; I studied them; I counted them; then I bowed to the third Paley as one bows to necessity. So far the thing was all within the limits of coincidence. It certainly seemed odd that this one particular cleric should be so varying and elusive. It was singular that Paley, alone among men, should swell and shrink and alter like a phantom, while all else remained solid. But the thing was explicable; two men had been ill and there was an end of it; only I went again the next night, and a clear-coloured elegant youth with powdered hair bounded up to me, and told me with boyish excitement that he was Paley.

For the next twenty-four hours I remained in the mental condition of the modern world. I mean the condition in which all natural explanations have broken down and no supernatural explanation has been established. My bewilderment had reached to boredom when I found myself once more in the colour and clatter of the pageant, and I was all the more pleased because I met an old school-fellow, and we mutually recognised each other under our heavy clothes and hoary wigs. We talked about all those great things for which literature is too small and only life large enough; red-hot memories and those gigantic details which make up the characters of men. I heard all about the friends he had lost sight of and those he had kept in sight; I heard about his profession, and asked at last how he came into the pageant.

"The fact is," he said, "a friend of mine asked me, just for to-night, to act a chap called Paley; I don't know who he was. . ."

"No, by thunder!" I said, "nor does anyone."

This was the last blow, and the next night passed like a dream. I scarcely noticed the slender, sprightly, and entirely new figure which fell into the ranks in the place of Paley, so many times deceased. What could it mean? Why was the giddy Paley unfaithful among the faithful found? Did these perpetual changes prove the popularity or the unpopularity of being Paley? Was it that no human being could support being Paley for one night and live till morning? Or was it that the gates were crowded with eager throngs of the British public thirsting to be Paley, who could only be let in one at a time? Or is there some ancient vendetta against Paley? Does some secret society of Deists still assassinate any one who adopts the name?

I cannot conjecture further about this true tale of mystery; and that for two reasons. First, the story is so true that I have had to put a lie into it. Every word of this narrative is veracious, except the one word Paley. And second, because I have got to go into the next room and dress up as Dr. Johnson.

A Note About the Author

G.K. Chesterton (1874–1936) is an English author, philosopher, and respected critic of literature and art. Chesterton was a very religious man, and was so interested in theology that he is considered a lay theologian. Much of his work dealt with topics of theology and philosophy. Chesterton became politically active during the last years of his life, advocating against both capitalism and socialism. With the inclusion of both religious and political philosophy, the G.K Chesterton made invaluable contributions to theology, economics, and literature.

A Note from the Publisher

Spanning many genres, from non-fiction essays to literature classics to children's books and lyric poetry, Mint Edition books showcase the master works of our time in a modern new package. The text is freshly typeset, is clean and easy to read, and features a new note about the author in each volume. Many books also include exclusive new introductory material. Every book boasts a striking new cover, which makes it as appropriate for collecting as it is for gift giving. Mint Edition books are only printed when a reader orders them, so natural resources are not wasted. We're proud that our books are never manufactured in excess and exist only in the exact quantity they need to be read and enjoyed.

bookfinity™

Discover more of your favorite classics with Bookfinity™.

- Track your reading with custom book lists.
- Get great book recommendations for your personalized Reader Type.
- Add reviews for your favorite books.
- AND MUCH MORE!

Visit **bookfinity.com** and take the fun Reader Type quiz to get started.

Enjoy our classic and modern companion pairings!

Classic & Modern

Bookfinity is a registered trademark of Ingram Book Group LLC. © 2023 Bookfinity. All rights reserved.

Printed in the USA
CPSIA information can be obtained
at www.ICGtesting.com
JSHW082350140824
68134JS00020B/1987